YOU...
H...

2018

♏

SCORPIO

CONTENTS

1 Introduction   7

2 The Essence of Scorpio
   Exploring the Personality of Scorpio the Scorpion   9

3 Scorpio on the Cusp   15

4 Scorpio and its Ascendants   17

5 The Moon and the Part it Plays in your Life   31

6 Moon Signs   35

7 Scorpio in Love   39

8 Venus: The Planet of Love   43

9 Venus through the Zodiac Signs   45

10 Scorpio: 2017 Diary Pages   49

11 Scorpio: 2018 Diary Pages   71

12 Scorpio: 2018 In Brief   72

13 Rising Signs for Scorpio   157

14 The Zodiac, Planets and Correspondences   159

INTRODUCTION

Your Personal Horoscopes have been specifically created to allow you to get the most from astrological patterns and the way they have a bearing on not only your zodiac sign, but nuances within it. Using the diary section of the book you can read about the influences and possibilities of each and every day of the year. It will be possible for you to see when you are likely to be cheerful and happy or those times when your nature is in retreat and you will be more circumspect. The diary will help to give you a feel for the specific 'cycles' of astrology and the way they can subtly change your day-to-day life. For example, when you see the sign ☿, this means that the planet Mercury is retrograde at that time. Retrograde means it appears to be running backwards through the zodiac. Such a happening has a significant effect on communication skills, but this is only one small aspect of how the Personal Horoscope can help you.

With Your Personal Horoscope the story doesn't end with the diary pages. It includes simple ways for you to work out the zodiac sign the Moon occupied at the time of your birth, and what this means for your personality. In addition, if you know the time of day you were born, it is possible to discover your Ascendant, yet another important guide to your personal make-up and potential.

Many readers are interested in relationships and in knowing how well they get on with people of other astrological signs. You might also be interested in the way you appear to very different sorts of individuals. If you are such a person, the section on Venus will be of particular interest. Despite the rapidly changing position of this planet, you can work out your Venus sign, and learn what bearing it will have on your life.

Using Your Personal Horoscope you can travel on one of the most fascinating and rewarding journeys that anyone can take – the journey to a better realisation of self.

THE ESSENCE OF SCORPIO

Exploring the Personality of Scorpio the Scorpion

(24TH OCTOBER – 22ND NOVEMBER)

What's in a sign?

To say that you are a little complicated and somewhat difficult to understand is probably a great understatement. The basic reason for this lies in the peculiar nature of Scorpio rulership. In terms of the elements, your zodiac sign is a Water sign. This makes you naturally emotional, deep, somewhat reserved and ever anxious to help those around you. As a direct contrast, classical astrologers always maintained that your planetary ruler was Mars. Mars is the planet of combat and aggression, being positive and dominant under most circumstances. So it can be judged from the start that there are great contradictions within the basic Scorpio nature.

It's a fact that many people are naturally cautious of Scorpio people. Perhaps this isn't surprising. Under most circumstances you appear to be quiet and peaceful, but the situation is a little like a smoking bomb. When it comes to defending yourself, or in particular those people who you see as being important to you, there is virtually no limit to which you would refuse to go. Generally speaking our ancient ancestors were extremely wise in terms of the names they gave to the different zodiac signs. Consider the apparently diminutive and retiring scorpion. It doesn't go looking for trouble and is generally happy to remain in the shadows. However, if it is provoked, or even attacked, it will take on adversaries many times its own size. It carries a barbed sting in its tail and will strike without any additional warning if necessary.

All the same, the Scorpio reputation may be a little undeserved. Yours is one of the most compassionate and caring of all the zodiac signs. When it comes to working on behalf of humanity, especially the oppressed, the sick or the disenfranchised, you show your true mettle. You cannot stand the thought of people suffering unjustifiably, which is why many of the great social reformers and even freedom fighters had the same zodiac sign as you do.

As a Scorpio you are likely to be intuitive (some would say psychic) and under most circumstances you are more than willing to follow that little voice inside yourself that tells you how to behave in any given situation.

Scorpio resources

Your nature is so very often understated that it might be said that your greatest resource is surprise. You have the ability to shock people constantly, even those who think they understand you perfectly well. This brings us back to the creature for which your zodiac sign is named. A scorpion is diminutive – and would represent a tasty snack for any would-be predator. However, it defies logic by standing its ground and fighting back. When it does, woe betide the aggressor that refuses to take account of its presence. And so it is with you. Quiet, even reserved, you tend to get on with your work. This you do efficiently and without undue fuss, approaching each task with the same methodical attitude. People often don't even realise that you are around. And then, when they least expect it, there you are!

The ability to surprise means that you often get on in life against heavy odds. In addition you have great resilience and fortitude. It is possible for you to continue to work long and hard under circumstances that would force others to retreat. Most Scorpio people would not consider themselves to be tough – in fact quite a few are positively neurotic when it comes to matters associated with their own health. Yet you can endure hardship well and almost always win through in the end.

It's true that you may not be quite as confident as you could be. If you were, people would notice you more and that would detract from that all-important element of surprise that makes you so formidable, and which is definitely the most important weapon in your armoury. However, it is clear that your greatest resource is compassion, and on those occasions when you really allow it to show, you display yourself as being one of the most important allies to your fellow men and women.

At a practical level you are more than capable and can often be expected to perform tasks that you haven't necessarily undertaken before. You have a deep intelligence and good powers to reason things out. Most important of all is a determination that no other zodiac sign can match.

Beneath the surface

This section of an account of the typical Scorpio nature could fill an entire book in itself because you are such a complicated person. However, there are certain advantages to being a Scorpio. For example, nobody is going to run away with the idea that you are basically uncomplicated and shallow. It ought to be clear enough to the dullest observer that there is a boiling, seething volcano bubbling away beneath the surface of almost every Scorpio subject.

You are often accused of having a slightly dark view of life, and it's true that many Scorpio people enjoy a rather morbid curiosity and are fascinated by subjects that make other people shudder. At the same time you could hardly be described as being one of life's natural optimists. Part of the reason for this lies in the fact that you have been disappointed in the past and may have arrived at the conclusion that to expect the worst is often the most sensible course of action. At least that way you are likely to mitigate some of the potential depression regarding failures in the future.

Although this way of thinking is somewhat faulty, it comes so naturally to the Scorpio subject that it actually works very well, though it has to be said that it might be responsible for a tendency to hold back on occasions.

Assessing the way your inner mind works is as difficult for you as it is for any outsider. Even individuals who have been friends for years will sometimes come desperately unstuck if they arrive at the conclusion that they know well what makes you tick. In the recesses of your mind you are passionate, driving, restless, dissatisfied and frequently disappointed with your own efforts. On the other hand, you have the power to make dreams into realities and are excellent at hatching plans that will benefit people far from your own circle and circumstances. Being a tireless worker on behalf of the oppressed, the fate of humanity as a whole is ever an inner concern.

When you love you do so with great width and depth. Your capacity for jealousy knows no bounds and there are times when you can be as destructive to yourself as you ever could be regarding any other individual. Yet for all this your inner mind is lofty and can soar like an eagle on occasions. If the world at large was able to fathom just one tenth of the way your inner mind actually works, people would find you even more fascinating than they do already. But perhaps it's best that they don't. The deepest recesses of Scorpio are an intense secret and will usually stay that way.

11

Making the best of yourself

It isn't hard to find a single word that describes the way you can make the best of yourself, especially when viewed by the world at large. That word is 'communication'. When difficulties arise in your life, especially concerning other people, it's usually because you haven't managed to get your message across, and probably because you haven't even tried to do so. There is much to your nature that is electric, powerful and magnetic. These qualities make you potentially popular and fascinating to a wealth of individuals. Hide these qualities beneath too brusque an exterior and you can seem dark and brooding.

Of course it's a fine line and one that isn't easy to walk. You are constantly worried that if you show people what really makes you tick, they will not find you interesting at all. In reality this concern is totally without foundation. There is more than enough depth about you to last several lifetimes. It doesn't matter how much you give of yourself to the world at large, there are always going to be surprises galore to follow.

Use the dynamic qualities of your nature to the full. Traditionally your ruling planet is Mars – a real go-getter of a planetary ruler and one that imbues you with tremendous power to get things done at a practical level. On the way you need to show how much you care about others. Amidst a plethora of gifts offered to you by the celestial spheres, your ability to help others is likely to be top of the list. When you are giving you are also usually approachable. For you the two go hand in hand. Avoid allowing yourself to become morose or inward looking and always strive to find simple answers to simple questions.

Stick to some sort of work that you find interesting. That can be almost anything to a Scorpio, as long as it feeds the inner you. It does need to carry a degree of diversity and should ideally have an end product that is easy to see. On your journey through life don't get carried away with daydreams – yet on the other hand avoid losing your great potential to make them come true.

The impressions you give

This is one area of your life over which you do have a great deal of control. If the adage 'what you see is what you get' turns out to be true for many signs of the zodiac, it certainly isn't the case with you. The complexity of your nature makes it difficult for even you to find 'the real Scorpio', and in any case this tends to change from day to day. However, regarding some matters there isn't any doubt at all. Firstly you are deeply magnetic and possess the ability to arouse an instinctive fascination in others. Ally this to your propensity for being very positive in your decision making and you have a potentially formidable combination.

Most people already think of you as being an extremely interesting person. Unfortunately they may also occasionally consider you to be a little cool and somewhat difficult to approach. Neither of these impressions are true, it's simply that you are quite shy at heart, and sometimes find it difficult to believe that you could be liked by certain individuals. Learn to throw this erroneous assumption out of the window, and instead, expect to be viewed positively. To do so would make all the difference and would clear the way so that your more personable side can show all the time.

Very few people who know you well could fail to realise that you care deeply, especially about the well-being of the oppressed. You have a truly noble spirit, a fact that shines through in practically everything you do – yet another reason to be noticed.

It's true that you can sometimes make your secretive quality into an art form, which those looking in from the outside might find rather difficult to deal with. This represents another outward aspect of your nature that could so easily be altered. By all means keep your secrets, though not about matters that are of no real note whatsoever. In a single phrase, try to lighten up a little. It's all you need to be almost perfect!

13

The way forward

It must first be held in mind that Scorpio people are complicated. That's something you simply cannot get away from, no matter how much you might try. On the one hand you can deal with practical matters almost instinctively. You are resourceful, deep thinking, intense and fascinating. On the other side of the coin you are often too fond of luxury and will frequently withdraw yourself from situations that you do not care to pursue. You can be quite stubborn and can even bear a grudge if you feel that you have been provoked.

It is suggested in astrology that no quality of nature is necessarily good or bad, it really depends on the way it is used. For example, stubbornness can be considered a terrible fault, but not if you were being awkward concerning the obvious rights of an oppressed person or group. It turns out that Scorpio has more of a potential to be 'saint or sinner' than any zodiac sign. As long as you examine your motives in any given situation, whilst at the same time trying to cultivate a degree of flexibility that is not one of your natural gifts, then you won't go far wrong.

Turn on the charm when it is necessary because it will rarely if ever let you down. Think about the way you can serve the world, but don't preach about it. Love sincerely, but don't allow jealousy to spoil things. Be constructive in your determination and don't get on your high horse when it isn't necessary. Follow these simple rules for the best chance of progress.

Of course there are many positives around to start with. You are a very loyal friend, are capable of being extremely brave and tend to be very committed to family members. At the same time you are trustworthy and can work long and hard using your own initiative. Although you sometimes worry about your health, you are more robust than most and can endure a high degree of hardship if necessary. You don't take kindly to criticism but can be flexible enough to accept it if you know it is intended for your own good.

Few people doubt your sincerity – that is, when they know what you believe. So it's important to lay your thoughts on the line right from the start. And even if you don't choose to treat the whole world as a friend, you are capable of gathering a little circle around you who would never let you down. Do make sure, however, that this 'inner group' isn't simply comprised of other Scorpios!

SCORPIO ON THE CUSP

Astrological profiles are altered for those people born at either the beginning or the end of a zodiac sign, or, more properly, on the cusps of a sign. In the case of Scorpio this would be on the 24th of October and for two or three days after, and similarly at the end of the sign, probably from the 20th to the 22nd of November.

The Libra Cusp – October 24th to 26th

You are probably generally considered to be a bright and breezy sort of character, with a great deal of enthusiasm for life. Despite this, few people would doubt that you are a shrewd operator, and that you know what you want and have a fairly good idea of how to go about getting it. Not everyone likes you as much as you would wish, but that's because the Libran side of your nature longs for popularity, while set against this is your deep Scorpio need to speak your mind, even when you know that other people might wish you did not indulge in this trait very frequently.

In love, you typify the split between these two signs. On the one hand you are passionate, sincere and intense, while on the other your Libran responses can cause a certain fickle sort of affection to show sometimes, probably to the confusion of those with whom you are involved at a personal level. Nevertheless, few people would find fault with your basic nature and there isn't much doubt that your heart is in the right place.

When it comes to career matters, you have a very fortunate combination. Scorpio can sometimes be accused of lacking diplomacy, but nothing could be further from the truth with Libra. As a result, you have what it takes in terms of determination but at the same time you are capable of seeing the point of view put forward by colleagues. You tend to rise to the top of the tree and, with your mixture of raw ability and humour that most of the world approves of, you can stay there.

You won't be the sort of person to make quite as many enemies as Scorpio taken alone might do, and you need the cut and thrust of the world much more than the retiring creature after whom your zodiac sign is named. Try not to be controversial and do your best to retain a sense of humour, which is essential to your well-being. Few would doubt the fact that your heart is in the right place and your creative potential could be second to none. Most important of all, you need the self-satisfaction that comes from living in the real world.

The Sagittarius Cusp – November 20th to 22nd

You can be a really zany character, with a love of life that is second to none. Add to this a penetrating insight, a razor-sharp wit and an instinctive intuition that is quite remarkable and we find in you a formidable person. It's true that not everyone understands what makes you tick, probably least of all yourself, but you strive to be liked and really do want to advertise your willingness to learn and to grow, which isn't always the province of Scorpio when taken alone. Your capacity for work knows no bounds, though you don't really like to get your hands dirty and would feel more content when telling others what to do.

In a career sense, you need to be in a position from which you are able to delegate. This is not because you are afraid of hard work yourself, far from it, but you possess a strong ability to see through problems and you are a natural director of others. Sales careers may interest you, or a position from which you can organise and arrange things. However, you hate to be tied down to one place for long, so you would be at your best when allowed to move around freely and do things in your own way.

You are a natural social reformer, mainly because you are sure that you know what is right and just. In the main you are correct in your assumptions, but there are occasions when you should realise that there is more than one form of truth. Perhaps you are not always quite as patient with certain individuals as you might be but these generally tend to be people who show traits of cruelty or cunning. As a family person, you care very much for the people who figure most prominently in your life. Sometimes you are a definite home bird, with a preference for what you know and love, but this is offset by a restless trend within your nature that often sends you off into the wide blue yonder, chasing rainbows that the Scorpio side of your nature doubts are even there. Few would doubt your charm, your magnetism, or your desire to get ahead in life in almost any way possible. You combine patience with genuine talent and make a loyal, interesting and entertaining friend or lover.

SCORPIO AND ITS ASCENDANTS

The nature of every individual on the planet is composed of the rich variety of zodiac signs and planetary positions that were present at the time of their birth. Your Sun sign, which in your case is Scorpio, is one of the many factors when it comes to assessing the unique person you are. Probably the most important consideration, other than your Sun sign, is to establish the zodiac sign that was rising over the eastern horizon at the time that you were born. This is your Ascending or Rising sign. Most popular astrology fails to take account of the Ascendant, and yet its importance remains with you from the very moment of your birth, through every day of your life. The Ascendant is evident in the way you approach the world, and so, when meeting a person for the first time, it is this astrological influence that you are most likely to notice first. Our Ascending sign essentially represents what we appear to be, while the Sun sign is what we feel inside ourselves.

The Ascendant also has the potential for modifying our overall nature. For example, if you were born at a time of day when Scorpio was passing over the eastern horizon (this would be around the time of dawn) then you would be classed as a double Scorpio. As such, you would typify this zodiac sign, both internally and in your dealings with others. However, if your Ascendant sign turned out to be a Fire sign, such as Aries, there would be a profound alteration of nature, away from the expected qualities of Scorpio.

One of the reasons why popular astrology often ignores the Ascendant is that it has always been rather difficult to establish. We have found a way to make this possible by devising an easy-to-use table, which you will find on page 157 of this book. Using this, you can establish your Ascendant sign at a glance. You will need to know your rough time of birth, then it is simply a case of following the instructions.

For those readers who have no idea of their time of birth it might be worth allowing a good friend, or perhaps your partner, to read through the section that follows this introduction. Someone who deals with you on a regular basis may easily discover your Ascending sign, even though you could have some difficulty establishing it for yourself. A good understanding of this component of your nature is essential if you want to be aware of that 'other person' who is responsible for the way you make contact with the world at large. Your Sun sign, Ascendant sign, and the other pointers in this book

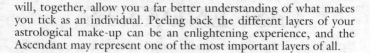

will, together, allow you a far better understanding of what makes you tick as an individual. Peeling back the different layers of your astrological make-up can be an enlightening experience, and the Ascendant may represent one of the most important layers of all.

Scorpio with Scorpio Ascendant

This is one of the most potent of all astrological possibilities, but how it is used depends so very much on the individual who possesses it. On the one hand you are magnetic, alluring, sexy, deep and very attractive, whilst at the same time you are capable of being stubborn, self-seeking, vain, over-sensitive and fathomless. It has to be said that under most circumstances the first set of adjectives are the most appropriate, and that is because you keep control of the deeper side, refusing to allow it absolute control over your conscious life. You are able to get almost anything you want from life, but first you have to discover what that might be. The most important factor of all, however, is the way you can offer yourself, totally and without reservation to a needy world.

Self-sacrifice is a marvellous thing, but you can go too far on occasions. The furthest extreme for Scorpios here is a life that is totally dedicated to work and prayer. For the few this is admirable, for the still earth-based, less so. Finding a compromise is not easy as you are not always in touch with yourself. Feed the spiritual, curb the excesses, accept the need for luxury, and be happy.

Scorpio with Sagittarius Ascendant

There are many gains with this combination, and most of you reading this will already be familiar with the majority of them. Sagittarius offers a bright and hopeful approach to life, but may not always have the staying power and the patience to get what it really needs. Scorpio, on the other hand, can be too deep for its own good, is very self-seeking on occasions and extremely giving to others. Both the signs have problems when taken on their own, and, it has to be said, double the difficulties when they come together. But this is not usually the case. Invariably the presence of Scorpio slows down the over-quick responses of the Archer, whilst the inclusion of Sagittarius prevents Scorpio from taking itself too seriously.

Life is so often a game of extremes, when all the great spiritual masters of humanity have indicated that a 'middle way' is the path to choose. You have just the right combination of skills and mental faculties to find that elusive path, and can bring great joy to yourself and others as a result. Most of the time you are happy, optimistic, helpful and a joy to know. You have mental agility, backed up by a stunning intuition, which itself would rarely let you down. Keep a sense of proportion and understand that your depth of intellect is necessary to curb your flighty side.

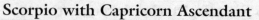

Scorpio with Capricorn Ascendant

If patience, perseverance and a solid ability to get where you want to go are considered to be the chief components of a happy life, then you should be skipping about every day. Unfortunately this is not always the case and here we have two zodiac signs, both of which can be too deep for their own good. Both Scorpio and Capricorn are inclined to take themselves rather too seriously and your main lesson in life, and some would say the reason you have adopted this zodiac combination, is to 'lighten up'. If all that determination is pushed in the direction of your service to the world at large, you are seen as being one of the kindest people imaginable. This is really the only option for you, because if you turn this tremendous potential power inwards all the time you will become brooding, secretive and sometimes even selfish. Your eyes should be turned towards a needy humanity, which can be served with the dry but definite wit of Capricorn and the true compassion of Scorpio.

It is impossible with this combination to indicate what areas of life suit you the best. Certainly you adore luxury in all its forms, and yet you can get by with almost nothing. You desire travel, and at the same time love the comforts and stability of home. The people who know you best are aware that you are rather special. Listen to what they say.

Scorpio with Aquarius Ascendant

Here we have a combination that shows much promise and a flexibility that allows many changes in direction, allied to a power to succeed, sometimes very much against all the odds. Aquarius lightens the load of the Scorpio mind, turning the depths into potential and making intuitive foresight into a means for getting on in life. There are depths here, because even airy Aquarius isn't too easy to understand, and it is therefore a fact that some people with this combination will always be something of a mystery. However, even this fact can be turned to your advantage because it means that people will always be looking at you. Confidence is so often the key to success in life and the Scorpio–Aquarius mix offers this, or at least appears to do so. Even when this is not entirely the case, the fact that everyone around you believes it to be true is often enough.

You are usually good to know, and show a keen intellect and a deep intelligence, aided by a fascination for life that knows no bounds. When at your best you are giving, understanding, balanced and active. On those occasions when things are not going well for you, beware a stubborn streak and the need to be sensational. Keep it light and happy and you won't go far wrong. Most of you are very, very well loved.

Scorpio with Pisces Ascendant

You stand a chance of disappearing so deep into yourself that other people would need one of those long ladders that cave explorers use, just to find you. It isn't really your fault because both Scorpio and Pisces are Water signs, which are difficult to understand, and you have them both. But that doesn't mean that you should be content to remain in the dark, and the warmth of your nature is all you need to shine a light on the wonderful qualities you possess. But the primary word of warning is that you must put yourself on display and allow others to know what you are, before their appreciation of these facts becomes apparent.

As a server of the world you are second to none and it is hard to find a person with this combination who is not, in some way, looking out for the people around them. Immensely attractive to others, you are also one of the most sought-after lovers. Much of this has to do with your deep and abiding charm, but the air of mystery that surrounds you also helps. Some of you will marry too early, and end up regretting the fact, though the majority of people with Scorpio and Pisces will find the love they deserve in the end. You are able, just, firm but fair, though a sucker for a hard luck story and as kind as the day is long. It's hard to imagine how so many good points could be ignored by others.

Scorpio with Aries Ascendant

The two very different faces of Mars come together in this potent, magnetic and quite awe-inspiring combination. Your natural inclination is towards secrecy, and this fact, together with the natural attractions of the sensual Scorpio nature, makes you the object of great curiosity. This means that you will not go short of attention and should ensure that you are always being analysed by people who may never get to know you at all. At heart you prefer your own company, and yet life appears to find means to push you into the public gaze time and again. Most people with this combination ooze sex appeal and can use this fact as a stepping stone to personal success, yet without losing any integrity or loosening the cords of a deeply moralistic nature.

On those occasions when you do lose your temper, there isn't a character in the length and breadth of the zodiac who would have either the words or the courage to stand against the stream of invective that follows. On really rare occasions you might even scare yourself. A simple look is enough to show family members when you are not amused. Few people are left unmoved by your presence in their life.

Scorpio with Taurus Ascendant

The first, last and most important piece of advice for you is not to take yourself, or anyone else, too seriously. This might be rather a tall order because Scorpio intensifies the deeper qualities of Taurus and can make you rather lacking in the sense of humour that we all need to live our lives in this most imperfect of worlds. You are naturally sensual by nature. This shows itself in a host of ways. In all probability you can spend hours in the bath, love to treat yourself to good food and drink and take your greatest pleasure in neat and orderly surroundings. This can often alienate you from those who live in the same house because other people need to use the bathroom from time to time and they cannot remain tidy indefinitely.

You tend to worry a great deal about things which are really not too important, but don't take this statement too seriously or you will begin to worry about this fact too! You often need to lighten up and should always do your best to tell yourself that most things are not half so important as they seem to be. Be careful over the selection of a life partner and if possible choose someone who is naturally funny and who does not take life anywhere near as seriously as you are inclined to do. At work you are more than capable and in all probability everyone relies heavily on your wise judgements.

Scorpio with Gemini Ascendant

What you are and what you appear to be can be two entirely different things with this combination. Although you appear to be every bit as chatty and even as flighty as Gemini tends to be, nothing could be further from the truth. In reality you have many deep and penetrating insights, all of which are geared towards sorting out potential problems before they come along. Few people would have the ability to pull the wool over your eyes, and you show a much more astute face to the world than is often the case for Gemini taken on its own. The level of your confidence, although not earth-shattering, is much greater with this combination, and you would not be thwarted once you had made up your mind.

There is a slight danger here, however, because Gemini is always inclined to nerve problems of one sort or another. In the main these are slight and fleeting, though the presence of Scorpio can intensify reactions and heighten the possibility of depression, which would not be at all fortunate. The best way round this potential problem is to have a wealth of friends, plenty to do and the sort of variety in your life that suits your Mercury ruler. Financial success is not too difficult to achieve because you can easily earn money and then manage to hold on to it.

Scorpio with Cancer Ascendant

There are few more endearing zodiac combinations than this one. Both signs are Watery in nature and show a desire to work on behalf of humanity as a whole. The world sees you as being genuinely caring, full of sympathy for anyone in trouble and always ready to lend a hand when it is needed. You are a loyal friend, a great supporter of the oppressed and a lover of home and family. In a work sense you are capable, and command respect from your colleagues, even though this comes about courtesy of your quiet competence and not as a result of anything that you might happen to say.

But we should not get too carried away with external factors, or the way that others see you. Inside you are a boiling pool of emotion. You feel more strongly, love more deeply and hurt more fully than any other combination of the Water signs. Even those who think they know you really well would get a shock if they could take a stroll around the deeper recesses of your mind. Although these facts are true, they may be rather beside the point because it is a fact that the truth of your passion, commitment and deep convictions may only surface fully half a dozen times in your life. The fact is that you are a very private person at heart and you don't know how to be any other way.

Scorpio with Leo Ascendant

A Leo with intensity, that's what you are. You are mad about good causes and would argue the hind leg off a donkey in defence of your many ideals. If you are not out there saving the planet you could just be at home in the bath, thinking up the next way to save humanity from its own worst excesses. In your own life, although you love little luxuries, you are sparing and frugal, yet generous as can be to those you take to. It's a fact that you don't like everyone, and of course the same is true in reverse. It might be easier for you to understand why you can dislike than to appreciate the reverse side of the coin, for your pride can be badly dented on occasions. Scorpio brings a tendency to have down spells, though the fact that Leo is also strongly represented in your nature should prevent them from becoming a regular part of your life.

It is important for you to learn how to forgive and forget, and there isn't much point in bearing a grudge because you are basically too noble to do so. If something goes wrong, kiss the situation goodbye and get on with the next interesting adventure, of which there are many in your life. Stop–start situations sometimes get in the way, but there are plenty of people around who would be only too willing to lend a helping hand.

Scorpio with Virgo Ascendant

This is intensity carried through to the absolute. If you have a problem, it is that you fail to externalise all that is going on inside that deep, bubbling cauldron that is your inner self. Realising what you are capable of is not a problem; these only start when you have to make it plain to those around you what you want. Part of the reason for this is that you don't always understand yourself. You love intensely and would do absolutely anything for a person you are fond of, even though you might have to inconvenience yourself a great deal on the way. Relationships can cause you slight problems however, since you need to associate with people who at least come somewhere near to understanding what makes you tick. If you manage to bridge the gap between yourself and the world that constantly knocks on your door, you show yourself to be powerful, magnetic and compulsive.

There are times when you definitely prefer to stay quiet, though you do have a powerful ability to get your message across when you think it is necessary to do so. There are people around who might think that you are a push-over but they could easily get a shock when you sense that the time is right to answer back. You probably have a very orderly house and don't care for clutter of any sort.

Scorpio with Libra Ascendant

There is some tendency for you to be far more deep than the average Libran would appear to be and for this reason it is crucial that you lighten up from time to time. Every person with a Scorpio quality needs to remember that there is a happy and carefree side to all events and your Libran quality should allow you to bear this in mind. Sometimes you try to do too many things at the same time. This is fine if you take the casual overview of Libra, but less sensible when you insist on picking the last bone out of every potential, as is much more the case for Scorpio.

When worries come along, as they sometimes will, be able to listen to what your friends have to say and also realise that they are more than willing to work on your behalf, if only because you are so loyal to them. You do have a quality of self-deception, but this should not get in the way too much if you combine the instinctive actions of Libra with the deep intuition of your Scorpio component.

Probably the most important factor of this combination is your ability to succeed in a financial sense. You make a good manager, but not of the authoritarian sort. Jobs in the media or where you are expected to make up your mind quickly would suit you, because there is always an underpinning of practical sense that rarely lets you down.

THE MOON AND THE PART IT PLAYS IN YOUR LIFE

In astrology the Moon is probably the single most important heavenly body after the Sun. Its unique position, as partner to the Earth on its journey around the solar system, means that the Moon appears to pass through the signs of the zodiac extremely quickly. The zodiac position of the Moon at the time of your birth plays a great part in personal character and is especially significant in the build-up of your emotional nature.

Your Own Moon Sign

Discovering the position of the Moon at the time of your birth has always been notoriously difficult because tracking the complex zodiac positions of the Moon is not easy. This process has been reduced to three simple stages with our Lunar Tables. A breakdown of the Moon's zodiac positions can be found from page 35 onwards, so that once you know what your Moon Sign is, you can see what part this plays in the overall build-up of your personal character.

If you follow the instructions on the next page you will soon be able to work out exactly what zodiac sign the Moon occupied on the day that you were born and you can then go on to compare the reading for this position with those of your Sun sign and your Ascendant. It is partly the comparison between these three important positions that goes towards making you the unique individual you are.

HOW TO DISCOVER YOUR MOON SIGN

This is a three-stage process. You may need a pen and a piece of paper but if you follow the instructions below the process should only take a minute or so.

STAGE 1 First of all you need to know the Moon Age at the time of your birth. If you look at Moon Table 1, on page 33, you will find all the years between 1920 and 2018 down the left side. Find the year of your birth and then trace across to the right to the month of your birth. Where the two intersect you will find a number. This is the date of the New Moon in the month that you were born. You now need to count forward the number of days between the New Moon and your own birthday. For example, if the New Moon in the month of your birth was shown as being the 6th and you were born on the 20th, your Moon Age Day would be 14. If the New Moon in the month of your birth came after your birthday, you need to count forward from the New Moon in the previous month. Whatever the result, jot this number down so that you do not forget it.

STAGE 2 Take a look at Moon Table 2 on page 34. Down the left hand column look for the date of your birth. Now trace across to the month of your birth. Where the two meet you will find a letter. Copy this letter down alongside your Moon Age Day.

STAGE 3 Moon Table 3 on page 34 will supply you with the zodiac sign the Moon occupied on the day of your birth. Look for your Moon Age Day down the left hand column and then for the letter you found in Stage 2. Where the two converge you will find a zodiac sign and this is the sign occupied by the Moon on the day that you were born.

Your Zodiac Moon Sign Explained

You will find a profile of all zodiac Moon Signs on pages 35 to 38, showing in yet another way how astrology helps to make you into the individual that you are. In each daily entry of the Astral Diary you can find the zodiac position of the Moon for every day of the year. This also allows you to discover your lunar birthdays. Since the Moon passes through all the signs of the zodiac in about a month, you can expect something like twelve lunar birthdays each year. At these times you are likely to be emotionally steady and able to make the sort of decisions that have real, lasting value.

MOON TABLE 1

YEAR	SEP	OCT	NOV	YEAR	SEP	OCT	NOV	YEAR	SEP	OCT	NOV
1920	12	12	10	1953	8	8	6	1986	4	3	2
1921	2	1/30	29	1954	27	26	25	1987	23	22	21
1922	21	20	19	1955	16	15	14	1988	11	10	9
1923	10	10	8	1956	4	4	2	1989	29	29	28
1924	28	28	26	1957	23	23	21	1990	19	18	17
1925	18	17	16	1958	13	12	11	1991	8	8	6
1926	7	6	5	1959	3	2/31	30	1992	26	25	24
1927	25	25	24	1960	21	20	19	1993	16	15	14
1928	14	14	12	1961	10	9	8	1994	5	5	3
1929	3	2	1	1962	28	28	27	1995	24	24	22
1930	22	20	19	1963	17	17	15	1996	13	11	10
1931	12	11	9	1964	6	5	4	1997	2	2/31	30
1932	30	29	27	1965	25	24	22	1998	20	20	19
1933	19	19	17	1966	14	14	12	1999	9	9	8
1934	9	8	7	1967	4	3	2	2000	27	27	26
1935	27	27	26	1968	23	22	21	2001	17	17	16
1936	15	15	14	1969	11	10	9	2002	6	6	4
1937	4	4	3	1970	1	1/30	29	2003	26	25	24
1938	23	23	22	1971	19	19	18	2004	13	12	11
1939	13	12	11	1972	8	8	6	2005	3	2	1
1940	2	1/30	29	1973	27	26	25	2006	22	21	20
1941	21	20	19	1974	16	15	14	2007	12	11	9
1942	10	10	8	1975	5	5	3	2008	30	29	28
1943	29	29	27	1976	23	23	21	2009	19	18	17
1944	17	17	15	1977	13	12	11	2010	8	8	6
1945	6	6	4	1978	2	2/31	30	2011	27	27	25
1946	25	24	23	1979	21	20	19	2012	6	15	13
1947	14	14	12	1980	10	9	8	2013	4	4	2
1948	3	2	1	1981	28	27	26	2014	23	22	22
1949	23	21	20	1982	17	17	15	2015	13	12	11
1950	12	11	9	1983	7	6	4	2016	1	30	29
1951	1	1/30	29	1984	25	24	22	2017	20	20	18
1952	19	18	17	1985	14	14	12	2018	9	9	7

TABLE 2   MOON TABLE 3

DAY	OCT	NOV	M/D	a	b	d	e	f	g	i
1	a	e	0	LI	LI	LI	SC	SC	SC	SA
2	a	e	1	LI	LI	SC	SC	SC	SA	SA
3	a	e	2	LI	SC	SC	SC	SA	SA	CP
4	b	f	3	SC	SC	SC	SA	SA	CP	CP
5	b	f	4	SC	SA	SA	SA	CP	CP	CP
6	b	f	5	SA	SA	SA	CP	CP	AQ	AQ
7	b	f	6	SA	CP	CP	CP	AQ	AQ	AQ
8	b	f	7	SA	CP	CP	AQ	AQ	PI	PI
9	b	f	8	CP	CP	CP	AQ	PI	PI	PI
10	b	f	9	CP	AQ	AQ	AQ	PI	PI	AR
11	b	f	10	AQ	AQ	AQ	PI	AR	AR	AR
12	b	f	11	AQ	PI	PI	PI	AR	AR	TA
13	b	g	12	PI	PI	PI	AR	TA	TA	TA
14	d	g	13	PI	AR	PI	AR	TA	TA	GE
15	d	g	14	AR	AR	AR	TA	GE	GE	GE
16	d	g	15	AR	AR	AR	TA	TA	TA	GE
17	d	g	16	AR	AR	TA	TA	GE	GE	GE
18	d	g	17	AR	TA	TA	GE	GE	GE	CA
19	d	g	18	TA	TA	GE	GE	GE	CA	CA
20	d	g	19	TA	TA	GE	GE	CA	CA	CA
21	d	g	20	GE	GE	GE	CA	CA	CA	LE
22	d	g	21	GE	GE	CA	CA	CA	LE	LE
23	d	i	22	GE	CA	CA	CA	LE	LE	VI
24	e	i	23	CA	CA	CA	LE	LE	LE	VI
25	e	i	24	CA	CA	LE	LE	LE	VI	VI
26	e	i	25	CA	LE	LE	LE	VI	VI	LI
27	e	i	26	LE	LE	VI	VI	VI	LI	LI
28	e	i	27	LE	VI	VI	VI	LI	LI	SC
29	e	i	28	VI	VI	VI	LI	LI	LI	SC
30	e	i	29	VI	VI	LI	LI	LI	SC	SC
31	e	–								

AR = Aries, TA = Taurus, GE = Gemini, CA = Cancer, LE = Leo, VI = Virgo,
LI = Libra, SC = Scorpio, SA = Sagittarius, CP = Capricorn, AQ = Aquarius, PI = Pisces

MOON SIGNS

Moon in Aries

You have a strong imagination, courage, determination and a desire to do things in your own way and forge your own path through life.

Originality is a key attribute; you are seldom stuck for ideas although your mind is changeable and you could take the time to focus on individual tasks. Often quick-tempered, you take orders from few people and live life at a fast pace. Avoid health problems by taking regular time out for rest and relaxation.

Emotionally, it is important that you talk to those you are closest to and work out your true feelings. Once you discover that people are there to help, there is less necessity for you to do everything yourself.

Moon in Taurus

The Moon in Taurus gives you a courteous and friendly manner, which means you are likely to have many friends.

The good things in life mean a lot to you, as Taurus is an Earth sign that delights in experiences which please the senses. Hence you are probably a lover of good food and drink, which may in turn mean you need to keep an eye on the bathroom scales, especially as looking good is also important to you.

Emotionally you are fairly stable and you stick by your own standards. Taureans do not respond well to change. Intuition also plays an important part in your life.

Moon in Gemini

You have a warm-hearted character, sympathetic and eager to help others. At times reserved, you can also be articulate and chatty: this is part of the paradox of Gemini, which always brings duplicity to the nature. You are interested in current affairs, have a good intellect, and are good company and likely to have many friends. Most of your friends have a high opinion of you and would be ready to defend you should the need arise. However, this is usually unnecessary, as you are quite capable of defending yourself in any verbal confrontation.

Travel is important to your inquisitive mind and you find intellectual stimulus in mixing with people from different cultures. You also gain much from reading, writing and the arts but you do need plenty of rest and relaxation in order to avoid fatigue.

Moon in Cancer

The Moon in Cancer at the time of birth is a fortunate position as Cancer is the Moon's natural home. This means that the qualities of compassion and understanding given by the Moon are especially enhanced in your nature, and you are friendly and sociable and cope well with emotional pressures. You cherish home and family life, and happily do the domestic tasks. Your surroundings are important to you and you hate squalor and filth. You are likely to have a love of music and poetry.

Your basic character, although at times changeable like the Moon itself, depends on symmetry. You aim to make your surroundings comfortable and harmonious, for yourself and those close to you.

Moon in Leo

The best qualities of the Moon and Leo come together to make you warm-hearted, fair, ambitious and self-confident. With good organisational abilities, you invariably rise to a position of responsibility in your chosen career. This is fortunate as you don't enjoy being an 'also-ran' and would rather be an important part of a small organisation than a menial in a large one.

You should be lucky in love, and happy, provided you put in the effort to make a comfortable home for yourself and those close to you. It is likely that you will have a love of pleasure, sport, music and literature. Life brings you many rewards, most of them as a direct result of your own efforts, although you may be luckier than average and ready to make the best of any situation.

Moon in Virgo

You are endowed with good mental abilities and a keen receptive memory, but you are never ostentatious or pretentious. Naturally quite reserved, you still have many friends, especially of the opposite sex. Marital relationships must be discussed carefully and worked at so that they remain harmonious, as personal attachments can be a problem if you do not give them your full attention.

Talented and persevering, you possess artistic qualities and are a good homemaker. Earning your honours through genuine merit, you work long and hard towards your objectives but show little pride in your achievements. Many short journeys will be undertaken in your life.

Moon in Libra

With the Moon in Libra you are naturally popular and make friends easily. People like you, probably more than you realise, you bring fun to a party and are a natural diplomat. For all its good points, Libra is not the most stable of astrological signs and, as a result, your emotions can be a little unstable too. Therefore, although the Moon in Libra is said to be good for love and marriage, your Sun sign and Rising sign will have an important effect on your emotional and loving qualities.

You must remember to relate to others in your decision-making. Co-operation is crucial because Libra represents the 'balance' of life that can only be achieved through harmonious relationships. Conformity is not easy for you because Libra, an Air sign, likes its independence.

Moon in Scorpio

Some people might call you pushy. In fact, all you really want to do is to live life to the full and protect yourself and your family from the pressures of life. Take care to avoid giving the impression of being sarcastic or impulsive and use your energies wisely and constructively.

You have great courage and you invariably achieve your goals by force of personality and sheer effort. You are fond of mystery and are good at predicting the outcome of situations and events. Travel experiences can be beneficial to you.

You may experience problems if you do not take time to examine your motives in a relationship, and also if you allow jealousy, always a feature of Scorpio, to cloud your judgement.

Moon in Sagittarius

The Moon in Sagittarius helps to make you a generous individual with humanitarian qualities and a kind heart. Restlessness may be intrinsic as your mind is seldom still. Perhaps because of this, you have a need for change that could lead you to several major moves during your adult life. You are not afraid to stand your ground when you know your judgement is right, you speak directly and have good intuition.

At work you are quick, efficient and versatile and so you make an ideal employee. You need work to be intellectually demanding and do not enjoy tedious routines.

In relationships, you anger quickly if faced with stupidity or deception, though you are just as quick to forgive and forget. Emotionally, there are times when your heart rules your head.

Moon in Capricorn

The Moon in Capricorn makes you popular and likely to come into the public eye in some way. The watery Moon is not entirely comfortable in the Earth sign of Capricorn and this may lead to some difficulties in the early years of life. An initial lack of creative ability and indecision must be overcome before the true qualities of patience and perseverance inherent in Capricorn can show through.

You have good administrative ability and are a capable worker, and if you are careful you can accumulate wealth. But you must be cautious and take professional advice in partnerships, as you are open to deception. You may be interested in social or welfare work, which suit your organisational skills and sympathy for others.

Moon in Aquarius

The Moon in Aquarius makes you an active and agreeable person with a friendly, easy-going nature. Sympathetic to the needs of others, you flourish in a laid-back atmosphere. You are broad-minded, fair and open to suggestion, although sometimes you have an unconventional quality which others can find hard to understand.

You are interested in the strange and curious, and in old articles and places. You enjoy trips to these places and gain much from them. Political, scientific and educational work interests you and you might choose a career in science or technology.

Money-wise, you make gains through innovation and concentration and Lunar Aquarians often tackle more than one job at a time. In love you are kind and honest.

Moon in Pisces

You have a kind, sympathetic nature, somewhat retiring at times, but you always take account of others' feelings and help when you can.

Personal relationships may be problematic, but as life goes on you can learn from your experiences and develop a better understanding of yourself and the world around you.

You have a fondness for travel, appreciate beauty and harmony and hate disorder and strife. You may be fond of literature and would make a good writer or speaker yourself. You have a creative imagination and may come across as an incurable romantic. You have strong intuition, maybe bordering on a mediumistic quality, which sets you apart from the mass. You may not be rich in cash terms, but your personal gifts are worth more than gold.

SCORPIO IN LOVE

Discover how compatible you are with people from the same and other parts of the zodiac. Five stars equals a match made in heaven!

Scorpio meets Scorpio

Scorpio is deep, complex and enigmatic, traits which often lead to misunderstanding with other zodiac signs, so a double Scorpio match can work well because both parties understand one another. They will allow each other periods of silence and reflection but still be willing to help, advise and support when necessary. Their relationship may seem odd to others but that doesn't matter if those involved are happy. All in all, an unusual but contented combination. Star rating: *****

Scorpio meets Sagittarius

Sagittarius needs constant stimulation and loves to be busy from dawn till dusk which may mean that it feels rather frustrated by Scorpio. Scorpions are hard workers, too, but they are also contemplative and need periods of quiet which may mean that they appear dull to Sagittarius. This could lead to a gulf between the two which must be overcome. With time and patience on both sides, this can be a lucrative encounter and good in terms of home and family. A variable alliance. Star rating: ***

Scorpio meets Capricorn

Lack of communication is the governing factor here. Neither of this pair are renowned communicators and both need a partner to draw out their full verbal potential. Consequently, Scorpio may find Capricorn cold and unapproachable while Capricorn could find Scorpio dark and brooding. Both are naturally tidy and would keep a pristine house but great effort and a mutual goal is needed on both sides to overcome the missing spark. A good match on the financial side, but probably not an earth-shattering personal encounter. Star rating: **

Scorpio meets Aquarius

This is a promising and practical combination. Scorpio responds well to Aquarius' exploration of its deep nature and so this shy sign becomes lighter, brighter and more inspirational. Meanwhile, Aquarians are rarely as sure of themselves as they like to appear and are reassured by Scorpio's steady and determined support. Both signs want to be kind to the other which is a basis for a relationship that should be warm most of the time and extremely hot occasionally. Star rating: ****

Scorpio meets Pisces

If ever there were two zodiac signs that have a total rapport, it has to be Scorpio and Pisces. They share very similar needs: they are not gregarious and are happy with a little silence, good music and time to contemplate the finer things in life, and both are attracted to family life. Apart, they can have a tendency to wander in a romantic sense, but this is reduced when they come together. They are deep, firm friends who enjoy each other's company and this must lead to an excellent chance of success. These people are surely made for each other! Star rating: *****

Scorpio meets Aries

There can be great affection here, even if the two signs are so very different. The common link is the planet Mars, which plays a part in both these natures. Although Aries is, outwardly, the most dominant, Scorpio people are among the most powerful to be found anywhere. This quiet determination is respected by Aries. Aries will satisfy the passionate side of Scorpio, particularly with instruction from Scorpio. There are mysteries here which will add spice to life. The few arguments that do occur are likely to be awe-inspiring. Star rating: ****

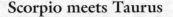

Scorpio meets Taurus

Scorpio is deep – very deep – which may be a problem, because Taurus doesn't wear its heart on its sleeve either. It might be difficult for this pair to get together, because neither is naturally inclined to make the first move. Taurus stands in awe of the power and intensity of the Scorpio mind, while the Scorpion is interested in the Bull's affable and friendly qualities, so an enduring relationship could be forged if the couple ever get round to talking. Both are lovers of home and family, which will help to cement a relationship. Star rating: **

Scorpio meets Gemini

There could be problems here. Scorpio is one of the deepest and least understood of all the zodiac signs, which at first seems like a challenge to intellectual Gemini, who thinks it can solve anything. But the deeper the Gemini digs, the further down Scorpio goes. Meanwhile, Scorpio may be finding Gemini thoughtless, shallow and even downright annoying. Gemini is often afraid of Scorpio's perception and strength, together with the sting in the Scorpion's tail. Anything is possible, but the outlook for this match is less than promising. Star rating: **

Scorpio meets Cancer

This match is potentially a great success, a fact which is often a mystery to astrologers. Some feel it is due to the compatibility of the Water element, but it could also come from a mixture of similarity and difference in the personalities. Scorpio is partly ruled by Mars, which gives it a deep, passionate, dominant and powerful side. Cancerians generally like and respect this amalgam, and recognise something there that they would like to adopt themselves. On the other side of the coin, Scorpio needs love and emotional security which Cancer offers generously. Star rating: *****

Scorpio meets Leo

Stand back and watch the sparks fly! Scorpio has the deep sensitivity of a Water sign but it is also partially ruled by Fire planet Mars, from which it draws great power, and Leo will find that difficult. Leo loves to take charge and really hates to feel psychologically undermined, which is Scorpio's stock-in-trade. Scorpio may find Leo's ideals a little shallow, which will be upsetting to the Lion. Anything is possible, but this possibility is rather slimmer than most. Star rating: **

Scorpio meets Virgo

There are one or two potential difficulties here, but there is also a meeting point from which to overcome them. Virgo is very caring and protective, a trait which Scorpio understands and even emulates. Scorpio will impress Virgo with its serious side. Both signs are consistent, although also sarcastic. Scorpio may uncover a hidden passion in Virgo which all too often lies deep within its Earth-sign nature. Material success is very likely, with Virgo taking the lion's share of the domestic chores and family responsibilities. Star rating: ***

Scorpio meets Libra

Many astrologers have reservations about this match because, on the surface, the signs are so different. However, this couple may find fulfilment because these differences mean that their respective needs are met. Scorpio needs a partner to lighten the load, which won't daunt Libra, while Libra looks for a steadfast quality which it doesn't possess, but which Scorpio can supply naturally. Financial success is possible because they both have good ideas and back them up with hard work and determination. All in all, a promising outlook. Star rating: ****

VENUS:
THE PLANET OF LOVE

If you look up at the sky around sunset or sunrise you will often see Venus in close attendance to the Sun. It is arguably one of the most beautiful sights of all and there is little wonder that historically it became associated with the goddess of love. But although Venus does play an important part in the way you view love and in the way others see you romantically, this is only one of the spheres of influence that it enjoys in your overall character.

Venus has a part to play in the more cultured side of your life and has much to do with your appreciation of art, literature, music and general creativity. Even the way you look is responsive to the part of the zodiac that Venus occupied at the start of your life, though this fact is also down to your Sun sign and Ascending sign. If, at the time you were born, Venus occupied one of the more gregarious zodiac signs, you will be more likely to wear your heart on your sleeve, as well as to be more attracted to entertainment, social gatherings and good company. If on the other hand Venus occupied a quiet zodiac sign at the time of your birth, you would tend to be more retiring and less willing to shine in public situations.

It's good to know what part the planet Venus plays in your life for it can have a great bearing on the way you appear to the rest of the world and since we all have to mix with others, you can learn to make the very best of what Venus has to offer you.

One of the great complications in the past has always been trying to establish exactly what zodiac position Venus enjoyed when you were born because the planet is notoriously difficult to track. However, we have solved that problem by creating a table that is exclusive to your Sun sign, which you will find on the following page.

Establishing your Venus sign could not be easier. Just look up the year of your birth on the next page and you will see a sign of the zodiac. This was the sign that Venus occupied in the period covered by your sign in that year. If Venus occupied more than one sign during the period, this is indicated by the date on which the sign changed, and the name of the new sign. For instance, if you were born in 1950, Venus was in Libra until the 28th October, after which time it was in Scorpio. If you were born before 28th October your Venus sign is Libra, if you were born on or after 28th October, your Venus sign is Scorpio. Once you have established the position of Venus at the time of your birth, you can then look in the pages which follow to see how this has a bearing on your life as a whole.

1920 SCORPIO / 24.10 SAGITTARIUS /
    17.11 CAPRICORN
1921 LIBRA / 14.11 SCORPIO
1922 SAGITTARIUS / 16.11 SCORPIO
1923 SCORPIO / 9.11 SAGITTARIUS
1924 VIRGO / 3.11 LIBRA
1925 SAGITTARIUS / 7.11 CAPRICORN
1926 LIBRA / 29.10 SCORPIO
1927 VIRGO / 10.11 LIBRA
1928 SAGITTARIUS /
    17.11 CAPRICORN
1929 LIBRA / 13.11 SCORPIO
1930 SAGITTARIUS / 16.11 SCORPIO
1931 SCORPIO / 8.11 SAGITTARIUS
1932 VIRGO / 2.11 LIBRA
1933 SAGITTARIUS / 7.11 CAPRICORN
1934 LIBRA / 29.10 SCORPIO
1935 VIRGO / 10.11 LIBRA
1936 SAGITTARIUS /
    16.11 CAPRICORN
1937 LIBRA / 13.11 SCORPIO
1938 SAGITTARIUS / 16.11 SCORPIO
1939 SCORPIO / 7.11 SAGITTARIUS
1940 VIRGO / 2.11 LIBRA
1941 SAGITTARIUS / 7.11 CAPRICORN
1942 LIBRA / 28.10 SCORPIO
1943 VIRGO / 10.11 LIBRA
1944 SAGITTARIUS /
    16.11 CAPRICORN
1945 LIBRA / 13.11 SCORPIO
1946 SAGITTARIUS / 16.11 SCORPIO
1947 SCORPIO / 6.11 SAGITTARIUS
1948 VIRGO / 1.11 LIBRA
1949 SAGITTARIUS / 6.11 CAPRICORN
1950 LIBRA / 28.10 SCORPIO
1951 VIRGO / 10.11 LIBRA
1952 SAGITTARIUS /
    16.11 CAPRICORN
1953 LIBRA / 12.11 SCORPIO
1954 SAGITTARIUS / 28.10 SCORPIO
1955 SCORPIO / 6.11 SAGITTARIUS
1956 VIRGO / 1.11 LIBRA
1957 SAGITTARIUS / 6.11 CAPRICORN
1958 LIBRA / 27.10 SCORPIO
1959 VIRGO / 10.11 LIBRA
1960 SAGITTARIUS /
    15.11 CAPRICORN
1961 LIBRA / 12.11 SCORPIO
1962 SAGITTARIUS / 28.10 SCORPIO
1963 SCORPIO / 5.11 SAGITTARIUS
1964 VIRGO / 31.10 LIBRA
1965 SAGITTARIUS / 6.11 CAPRICORN
1966 LIBRA / 27.10 SCORPIO
1967 VIRGO / 10.11 LIBRA
1968 SAGITTARIUS /
    15.11 CAPRICORN

1969 LIBRA / 11.11 SCORPIO
1970 SAGITTARIUS / 28.10 SCORPIO
1971 SCORPIO / 4.11 SAGITTARIUS
1972 VIRGO / 31.10 LIBRA
1973 SAGITTARIUS / 6.11 CAPRICORN
1974 LIBRA / 26.10 SCORPIO
1975 VIRGO / 9.11 LIBRA
1976 SAGITTARIUS /
    15.11 CAPRICORN
1977 LIBRA / 11.11 SCORPIO
1978 SAGITTARIUS / 28.10 SCORPIO
1979 SCORPIO / 4.11 SAGITTARIUS
1980 VIRGO / 30.10 LIBRA
1981 SAGITTARIUS / 5.11 CAPRICORN
1982 LIBRA / 26.10 SCORPIO
1983 VIRGO / 9.11 LIBRA
1984 SAGITTARIUS /
    14.11 CAPRICORN
1985 LIBRA / 10.11 SCORPIO
1986 SAGITTARIUS / 28.10 SCORPIO
1987 SCORPIO / 3.11 SAGITTARIUS
1988 VIRGO / 30.10 LIBRA
1989 SAGITTARIUS / 5.11 CAPRICORN
1990 LIBRA / 25.10 SCORPIO
1991 VIRGO / 9.11 LIBRA
1992 SAGITTARIUS /
    14.11 CAPRICORN
1993 LIBRA / 10.11 SCORPIO
1994 SAGITTARIUS / 28.10 SCORPIO
1995 SCORPIO / 3.11 SAGITTARIUS
1996 VIRGO / 29.10 LIBRA
1997 SAGITTARIUS / 5.11 CAPRICORN
1998 LIBRA / 25.10 SCORPIO
1999 VIRGO / 9.11 LIBRA
2000 SAGITTARIUS /
    14.11 CAPRICORN
2001 LIBRA / 10.11 SCORPIO
2002 SAGITTARIUS / 28.10 SCORPIO
2003 SCORPIO / 3.11 SAGITTARIUS
2004 VIRGO / 29.10 LIBRA
2005 SAGITTARIUS / 5.11 CAPRICORN
2006 LIBRA / 25.10 SCORPIO
2007 VIRGO / 9.11 LIBRA
2008 SAGITTARIUS /
    14.11 CAPRICORN
2009 LIBRA / 10.11 SCORPIO
2010 SAGITTARIUS / 28.10 SCORPIO
2011 SCORPIO / 3.11 SAGITTARIUS
2012 VIRGO / 29.10 LIBRA
2013 SAGITTARIUS / 5.11 CAPRICORN
2014 LIBRA / 25.10 SCORPIO
2015 VIRGO / 9.11 LIBRA
2016 SAGITTARIUS /
    13.11 CAPRICORN
2017 LIBRA / 10.11 SCORPIO
2018 SAGITTARIUS / 28.10 SCORPIO

VENUS THROUGH THE ZODIAC SIGNS

Venus in Aries

Amongst other things, the position of Venus in Aries indicates a fondness for travel, music and all creative pursuits. Your nature tends to be affectionate and you would try not to create confusion or difficulty for others if it could be avoided. Many people with this planetary position have a great love of the theatre, and mental stimulation is of the greatest importance. Early romantic attachments are common with Venus in Aries, so it is very important to establish a genuine sense of romantic continuity. Early marriage is not recommended, especially if it is based on sympathy. You may give your heart a little too readily on occasions.

Venus in Taurus

You are capable of very deep feelings and your emotions tend to last for a very long time. This makes you a trusting partner and lover, whose constancy is second to none. In life you are precise and careful and always try to do things the right way. Although this means an ordered life, which you are comfortable with, it can also lead you to be rather too fussy for your own good. Despite your pleasant nature, you are very fixed in your opinions and quite able to speak your mind. Others are attracted to you and historical astrologers always quoted this position of Venus as being very fortunate in terms of marriage. However, if you find yourself involved in a failed relationship, it could take you a long time to trust again.

Venus in Gemini

As with all associations related to Gemini, you tend to be quite versatile, anxious for change and intelligent in your dealings with the world at large. You may gain money from more than one source but you are equally good at spending it. There is an inference here that you are a good communicator, via either the written or the spoken word, and you love to be in the company of interesting people. Always on the look-out for culture, you may also be very fond of music, and love to indulge the curious and cultured side of your nature. In romance you tend to have more than one relationship and could find yourself associated with someone who has previously been a friend or even a distant relative.

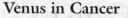

Venus in Cancer

You often stay close to home because you are very fond of family and enjoy many of your most treasured moments when you are with those you love. Being naturally sympathetic, you will always do anything you can to support those around you, even people you hardly know at all. This charitable side of your nature is your most noticeable trait and is one of the reasons why others are naturally so fond of you. Being receptive and in some cases even psychic, you can see through to the soul of most of those with whom you come into contact. You may not commence too many romantic attachments but when you do give your heart, it tends to be unconditionally.

Venus in Leo

It must become quickly obvious to almost anyone you meet that you are kind, sympathetic and yet determined enough to stand up for anyone or anything that is truly important to you. Bright and sunny, you warm the world with your natural enthusiasm and would rarely do anything to hurt those around you, or at least not intentionally. In romance you are ardent and sincere, though some may find your style just a little overpowering. Gains come through your contacts with other people and this could be especially true with regard to romance, for love and money often come hand in hand for those who were born with Venus in Leo. People claim to understand you, though you are more complex than you seem.

Venus in Virgo

Your nature could well be fairly quiet no matter what your Sun sign might be, though this fact often manifests itself as an inner peace and would not prevent you from being basically sociable. Some delays and even the odd disappointment in love cannot be ruled out with this planetary position, though it's a fact that you will usually find the happiness you look for in the end. Catapulting yourself into romantic entanglements that you know to be rather ill-advised is not sensible, and it would be better to wait before you committed yourself exclusively to any one person. It is the essence of your nature to serve the world at large and through doing so it is possible that you will attract money at some stage in your life.

Venus in Libra

Venus is very comfortable in Libra and bestows upon those people who have this planetary position a particular sort of kindness that is easy to recognise. This is a very good position for all sorts of friendships and also for romantic attachments that usually bring much joy into your life. Few individuals with Venus in Libra would avoid marriage and since you are capable of great depths of love, it is likely that you will find a contented personal life. You like to mix with people of integrity and intelligence but don't take kindly to scruffy surroundings or work that means getting your hands too dirty. Careful speculation, good business dealings and money through marriage all seem fairly likely.

Venus in Scorpio

You are quite open and tend to spend money quite freely, even on those occasions when you don't have very much. Although your intentions are always good, there are times when you get yourself in to the odd scrape and this can be particularly true when it comes to romance, which you may come to late or from a rather unexpected direction. Certainly you have the power to be happy and to make others contented on the way, but you find the odd stumbling block on your journey through life and it could seem that you have to work harder than those around you. As a result of this, you gain a much deeper understanding of the true value of personal happiness than many people ever do, and are likely to achieve true contentment in the end.

Venus in Sagittarius

You are lighthearted, cheerful and always able to see the funny side of any situation. These facts enhance your popularity, which is especially high with members of the opposite sex. You should never have to look too far to find romantic interest in your life, though it is just possible that you might be too willing to commit yourself before you are certain that the person in question is right for you. Part of the problem here extends to other areas of life too. The fact is that you like variety in everything and so can tire of situations that fail to offer it. All the same, if you choose wisely and learn to understand your restless side, then great happiness can be yours.

Venus in Capricorn

The most notable trait that comes from Venus in this position is that it makes you trustworthy and able to take on all sorts of responsibilities in life. People are instinctively fond of you and love you all the more because you are always ready to help those who are in any form of need. Social and business popularity can be yours and there is a magnetic quality to your nature that is particularly attractive in a romantic sense. Anyone who wants a partner for a lover, a spouse and a good friend too would almost certainly look in your direction. Constancy is the hallmark of your nature and unfaithfulness would go right against the grain. You might sometimes be a little too trusting.

Venus in Aquarius

This location of Venus offers a fondness for travel and a desire to try out something new at every possible opportunity. You are extremely easy to get along with and tend to have many friends from varied backgrounds, classes and inclinations. You like to live a distinct sort of life and gain a great deal from moving about, both in a career sense and with regard to your home. It is not out of the question that you could form a romantic attachment to someone who comes from far away or be attracted to a person of a distinctly artistic and original nature. What you cannot stand is jealousy, for you have friends of both sexes and would want to keep things that way.

Venus in Pisces

The first thing people tend to notice about you is your wonderful, warm smile. Being very charitable by nature you will do anything to help others, even if you don't know them well. Much of your life may be spent sorting out situations for other people, but it is very important to feel that you are living for yourself too. In the main, you remain cheerful, and tend to be quite attractive to members of the opposite sex. Where romantic attachments are concerned, you could be drawn to people who are significantly older or younger than yourself or to someone with a unique career or point of view. It might be best for you to avoid marrying whilst you are still very young.

SCORPIO:
2017 DIARY PAGES

October

2017

1 SUNDAY
Moon Age Day 11   Moon Sign Aquarius

Today you should feel freer to express yourself – in some cases perhaps too much so. Don't forget you are dealing with the feelings and emotions of those you care for the most. Being outspoken is all well and good but you shouldn't lose sight of your sense of responsibility. Stand by for new relationships to commence.

2 MONDAY
Moon Age Day 12   Moon Sign Aquarius

Apart from the happiness you are getting from personal relationships at the moment there isn't a great deal of sense that you are getting very far in the competitive world. Perhaps you need to give your more practical and professional life something of a boost? There are opportunities to do so if you keep looking.

3 TUESDAY
Moon Age Day 13   Moon Sign Pisces

Feeling yourself to be amongst just the right sort of company is what today is about. You are now more perceptive than usual and know where to go to get just the right sort of assistance. Where you really gain today, however, is in one-to-one relationships, especially with your partner. Romance is calling – can't you hear it?

4 WEDNESDAY
Moon Age Day 14   Moon Sign Pisces

The general routines of life could keep you busy today if you allow them to do so. If you want any change and diversity, you will have to go out and search for it. Favourable times are approaching in a financial sense and so take the time to look carefully at new ways of earning more money.

5 THURSDAY
Moon Age Day 15   Moon Sign Aries

A sense of team spirit could be lacking and that is part of what you have to put back into your life as soon as you can. There are people out there with whom you could really co-operate, plus a few individuals who have it in their power to boost your success rate. This is definitely a day to keep your eyes open.

6 FRIDAY
Moon Age Day 16   Moon Sign Aries

Although today is certainly not a time for grandiose plans, when it comes to the daily routines of life you appear to be getting on fine. However, you may soon notice that what is missing is excitement. Don't worry about this as the time isn't right for that yet and a few quieter days lay ahead. If you accept this fact you will enjoy today and the weekend more.

7 SATURDAY
Moon Age Day 17   Moon Sign Taurus

There is a possibility that you are even less enthusiastic than you intended to be today. All of a sudden it could feel as though everyone is relying solely on you and that is not a state of affairs you presently relish. Actually it's all a matter of perspective. In more positive times you would relish the attention.

8 SUNDAY
Moon Age Day 18   Moon Sign Taurus

The presence of the lunar low indicates that you should keep life as simple as possible this Sunday. Although the chilly winds might be on the way it wouldn't do any harm at all to get a little fresh air and a change of scene. Failing this, find some quiet and yet rewarding way to while away a few hours, possibly amongst family members.

9 MONDAY
Moon Age Day 19   Moon Sign Taurus

Make sure others don't get hold of the wrong end of the stick merely by explaining yourself carefully at present. Your attitude is one of armed neutrality at the moment, so others could find you to be somewhat aggressive. Settle down and spend some time with people you both like and trust.

10 TUESDAY · *Moon Age Day 20 · Moon Sign Gemini*

The emphasis now sits squarely on having fun and being able to express yourself fully. Trends have moved on and some of the less favourable days of earlier in the month are gone and finished. Your attitude tends to be one of optimism, which is a big part of what you need to feel happy with your lot.

11 WEDNESDAY · *Moon Age Day 21 · Moon Sign Gemini*

Your social environment contains more than a few interesting encounters that you would find particularly interesting during this midweek period. Some of these you are creating for yourself. This might be a favourable day to host a dinner party, or simply to go out in the evening with friends. Expect some admirers to gather round.

12 THURSDAY · *Moon Age Day 22 · Moon Sign Cancer*

There is just a slight possibility that you will now be overlooking a number of details in your short and medium-term planning. Try to take a wider view and see the whole picture if you can and where you experience some difficulty, try to seek the support of others. Spread difficult tasks out across the day and don't overload yourself at any one time.

13 FRIDAY · *Moon Age Day 23 · Moon Sign Cancer*

Your assessment of a personal situation could appear to be flawed in some way. The best time for thinking deeply about the more intimate aspects of your life would be in a few days from now. For today, it would seem to be sensible to adopt a casual attitude to life and to enjoy as much time with friends as you can manage.

14 SATURDAY · *Moon Age Day 24 · Moon Sign Leo*

Along comes a good period for exploring different possibilities, plus the chance to do rather better in the financial stakes. The more change you bring into your life at this time, the sooner you will get out of the doldrums and back into the trade winds of life. Throw around a few compliments and see what happens.

15 SUNDAY
Moon Age Day 25   Moon Sign Leo

In terms of self-expression you are likely to be a good deal more ebullient right now than you usually are, which means exercising a little self-control if you don't want that Scorpio outspokenness to get you into trouble. Not everyone seems to be especially helpful and you can expect to have to work hard on your own behalf now.

16 MONDAY
Moon Age Day 26   Moon Sign Virgo

This should be a very good time for getting along with others, in almost any potential situation. Don't be too shy to put your point of view forward, even in situations that are not familiar to you. It is very unlikely that your opinions would be derided at the moment and, on the contrary, you could make new allies.

17 TUESDAY
Moon Age Day 27   Moon Sign Virgo

It looks as though this is a period during which you can spend some time thinking about personal matters that need special attention. With a slight pause in the general forward momentum of life and a contemplative mood coming upon you, fairly lengthy periods of concentrated pondering are indicated. Enjoy this small window of introspection.

18 WEDNESDAY
Moon Age Day 28   Moon Sign Libra

When it comes to most aspects of life at the moment, you appear to want to have your cake and eat it too. Who wouldn't, but it really isn't possible for most of the time. Be content with your lot, whilst at the same time hanging on to those aspirations for the future. Only remember that life doesn't owe any of us a living.

19 THURSDAY
Moon Age Day 29   Moon Sign Libra

There is plenty of scope for mutual assistance and a general sense of harmony now. Although you are still inclined to be somewhat pensive, you should also discover that your curiosity is raised significantly. This can lead to you digging and delving, which means more communication with the world in general.

20 FRIDAY   *Moon Age Day 0   Moon Sign Libra*

With less scope for influencing others today, you tend to retreat into your own little world again. There isn't really much alternative because the Moon is in your twelfth house, where your Sun is already residing. The results are temporary and certainly not negative, though friends might think you are down in the dumps.

21 SATURDAY   *Moon Age Day 1   Moon Sign Scorpio*

With the Moon moving back into your zodiac sign today you can expect a fairly active and generally quite helpful weekend. You may see this time as being your last big chance to do something grand before the winter sets in. If this is the case then you will want to spread your wings. Do so in the company of those you really like.

22 SUNDAY   *Moon Age Day 2   Moon Sign Scorpio*

This Sunday looks dynamic and very interesting. It's time to push your way to the front of the queue. This doesn't mean having to fall out with anyone but merely expresses your present desire to get things done in the least complicated manner. Your creative potential should also be especially good.

23 MONDAY   *Moon Age Day 3   Moon Sign Sagittarius*

This is a time for staying on the move, something you will certainly enjoy now. Don't allow yourself to be held back, especially at those times when you have made up your mind to a particular course of action. Messy jobs, or those that you simply don't fancy, are likely to be delegated with ease today while you move on to more attractive tasks.

24 TUESDAY   *Moon Age Day 4   Moon Sign Sagittarius*

A boost to all matters associated with communication comes along and you feel the wind of change blowing. Get on with jobs that have been waiting for a while and don't allow yourself to be restricted by people who have a vested interest in holding you back. The charitable side of your nature is on display now.

25 WEDNESDAY   *Moon Age Day 5   Moon Sign Sagittarius*

There may not be many opportunities to have your ego massaged today but you simply have to get on and do things all the same. There could be difficulty in deciding how you want to spend your free time, especially during a period when practically everyone in the family is trying to attract your attention.

26 THURSDAY   *Moon Age Day 6   Moon Sign Capricorn*

A phase of dynamism and activity is at hand. Go for gold today and make certain that absolutely everyone knows who you are and what you want from life. Your chart today reveals that you are entertaining, keen to talk to almost anyone and anxious to let the world know what you believe about a host of issues.

27 FRIDAY   *Moon Age Day 7   Moon Sign Capricorn*

It should be possible, if not easy, to make some really good progress today, especially if you are at work. In other areas, friends might appear distant, or even awkward, which could lead to you having to analyse their possible problems. Fortunately, your tolerance level is extremely high at the present time, as is your desire to help.

28 SATURDAY   *Moon Age Day 8   Moon Sign Aquarius*

Emotional relationships are potentially good, but there is a danger that they could be beset by a few misunderstandings. It is very important to make sure that your partner or others you care about deeply understand you. This ought to pose no real problem because your powers of communication are extremely good now.

29 SUNDAY   *Moon Age Day 9   Moon Sign Aquarius*

This Sunday marks a high-spirited period and one during which you are laying down a few plans for later in the week. A few of the slightly negative planetary positions of recent times are now disappearing, so it could feel as if you have been released from a sort of straightjacket. Socially, it's time to rock.

30 MONDAY
Moon Age Day 10   Moon Sign Pisces

News you might have been expecting regarding a personal matter could fail to materialise. If so, you will simply have to show how patient you can be and it should come along in due course. Be sure to keep confidences because you won't be thought of any better if it appears that you are giving away the secrets of a friend.

31 TUESDAY
Moon Age Day 11   Moon Sign Pisces

There could be some unaccountable mishaps at home, which you will want to deal with as quickly as possible. Don't get strung up today with details but concentrate instead on the matter at hand. In work situations you tend to give a good account of yourself and it is possible that you could make some new allies.

November

2017

1 WEDNESDAY
Moon Age Day 12   Moon Sign Pisces

Now the temptation to empty your pocket on expensive things that you don't require could be quite strong. Before every proposed purchase stop and think carefully and then decide whether this is something you actually do need. As a result of some more positive trends, there could be some startling new ideas around now and you will want to go for them all.

2 THURSDAY
Moon Age Day 13   Moon Sign Aries

Show some patience, particularly with regard to people who can be irritating in the extreme. It won't help to lose your temper but it would be very good indeed if, instead, you could find people marvelling at your tolerance. Try to keep away from meaningless and boring routines if you can, as these will only cause you a sense of aggravation at present.

3 FRIDAY
Moon Age Day 14   Moon Sign Aries

Along comes a period during which you can pick up some significant information. It's time to pay great attention, even to apparently casual remarks. You will be amazed at your own resourcefulness and at your ability to make a silk purse out of a sow's ear. Almost everyone is keen to be your friend now.

4 SATURDAY
Moon Age Day 15   Moon Sign Taurus

Although this is the time of the lunar low, such is the power and influence of a number of important planetary positions now, that you will barely notice the slowdown that is usually the inevitable result. Keep plugging away in your efforts to get ahead but accept that your progress is likely to be hindered somewhat and don't allow this to depress you.

5 SUNDAY
Moon Age Day 16   Moon Sign Taurus

It is possible that you find you are running out of steam. Since this is a Sunday, which is usually referred to as being a day of rest, why not take notice of the fact and have a rest? If this proves to be impossible you could at least devote a few hours to social matters and to mixing freely with your friends.

6 MONDAY
Moon Age Day 17   Moon Sign Gemini

Partnerships are likely to take up a great deal of your time as you You seem to be in a commanding position with regard to the personality stakes. People gravitate towards you and your popularity is at a peak. Make the most of these trends by socialising freely and by maintaining a high profile at work. Monday morning blues are much less likely for you than they are for your family and friends. Be supportive if others need you to be.

7 TUESDAY
Moon Age Day 18   Moon Sign Gemini

Now your find yourself in a period during which forward planning is not only possible, but also enjoyable too. Although this isn't going to be a crackerjack of a day it does offer some particularly good prospects money-wise. Despite this you should avoid spending too much, except when you come across a bargain.

8 WEDNESDAY
Moon Age Day 19   Moon Sign Cancer

Some matters come to a head now. If you were a salesperson the advice would be 'to close deals carefully'. There is nothing wrong with your mental faculties but you may have to think carefully before taking specific steps. Keep up the social integration and listen to what all sorts of people have to say.

9 THURSDAY
Moon Age Day 20   Moon Sign Cancer

Significant input into areas of life you have stayed away from recently now seems to be the order of the day. You are almost certainly going to be busy today and will have little time to spare for frivolities. When it comes to the boring routines, see if you can find someone to lend a hand and make them more fun.

10 FRIDAY
Moon Age Day 21   Moon Sign Leo

Once more minor opportunities for financial gain pay you a visit. Keep an eye on what you are spending but at the same time understand that you have to speculate a little in order to accumulate later on. Think very carefully before you take any financial risks though. Rewards of a social nature may also come your way, probably because you are so kind at present.

11 SATURDAY
Moon Age Day 22   Moon Sign Leo

The material side of life should be offering everything you need, even if it isn't so easy to get everything you actually want. The weekend is likely to be variable, with perhaps some odd occurrences at times. Further your long-term ambitions by seeking out the right people and chatting to them at some stage today.

12 SUNDAY
Moon Age Day 23   Moon Sign Virgo

The recent planetary thrust has been towards fulfilling your desire for luxury, something that is endemic to the zodiac sign of Scorpio. In your current mood, be careful that you don't end up being accused of hedonism. In the main, you are sociable at the moment and should be mixing freely and happily with all manner of people.

13 MONDAY
Moon Age Day 24   Moon Sign Virgo

A revised plan of action at work could come along today and this could prove to be very timely indeed. Get everything sorted out at work and deal with all those little matters that have been left undone in recent days. By the evening you will be ready to have fun and this should not be hard to find.

14 TUESDAY
Moon Age Day 25   Moon Sign Libra

Finances are likely to be strengthened and you may be able to spend a little more freely than would often be the case. Plans put in place now should work well later, especially with regard to a journey you intend to make months from now. Patience is the key to success and offers great gains – though not for a while yet.

15 WEDNESDAY   *Moon Age Day 26   Moon Sign Libra*

You enjoy a very independent approach to life right now. This is fine, just as long as you don't give those around you the impression that you don't want their advice at all. Listen carefully to what you are being told but then go ahead and do what you wish – though as diplomatically as you can manage.

16 THURSDAY   *Moon Age Day 27   Moon Sign Libra*

You can open certain doors towards progress at this stage of November. With the Sun still in your first house and everything to play for after a less progressive phase, life should seem fairly fast in pace. Act on impulse, but only when your instincts tell you that this is the right way forward.

17 FRIDAY   *Moon Age Day 28   Moon Sign Scorpio*

Decision-making should turn out to be far easier now. The lunar high is very supportive when it comes to mixing with people you know can be good for you. Better luck is on the way and you should be able to indulge yourself in the odd speculation, as long as the risk is calculated.

18 SATURDAY   *Moon Age Day 0   Moon Sign Scorpio*

The lunar high continues to support your efforts to get ahead. These may be somewhat curtailed on a Saturday and professional issues especially might have to wait. That doesn't prevent you from having fun, or from making the most favourable impression imaginable on all types of people.

19 SUNDAY   *Moon Age Day 1   Moon Sign Sagittarius*

This can be a period of sudden emotional impulses, most of which won't be of any real use to you. Try to stay on an even keel and don't blow up simply because things are not necessarily going your way. Secrets coming your way may be important and you must keep the confidences that others place in you absolutely to yourself.

20 MONDAY   *Moon Age Day 2   Moon Sign Sagittarius*

Scorpio presently exhibits genuine intelligence and strong acumen when it comes to practical and financial matters. Some may call you ingenious in your handling of business situations. This could lead to a week of potential gains, although it may also leave you short of rest. Balance is everything in life.

21 TUESDAY   *Moon Age Day 3   Moon Sign Sagittarius*

A few minor disappointments in your love life are possible during this part of the working week. Don't allow these to dominate your thinking. What's needed today is a cool head and strong rational thought. Where you do recognise a few problems, time and your own changing attitude should put matters right.

22 WEDNESDAY   *Moon Age Day 4   Moon Sign Capricorn*

Energy is not lacking and neither is the ability to size up a situation and act immediately. With reactions like lightning and a strong ability to see 'clear through' the minds of those around you, it might be said that Scorpio is more potent now than has been the case at any time during the year. Make the most of these trends.

23 THURSDAY   *Moon Age Day 5   Moon Sign Capricorn*

This is a very favourable moment for putting new plans into action. The message is, don't delay. Money matters are simpler to deal with and life carries fewer complications than might have seemed to be the case over the last week or two. Try to avoid unnecessary spats at home, even if you are not the one starting them.

24 FRIDAY   *Moon Age Day 6   Moon Sign Aquarius*

All of a sudden, your thinking could appear somewhat muddled and your view of the future less focused. Don't panic. As the Moon progresses through your solar third house, you simply need some time off to communicate with those around you and to still your inner mind during what is quite a hectic phase.

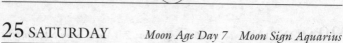

25 SATURDAY   *Moon Age Day 7   Moon Sign Aquarius*

If you want to find some relaxation today, look towards home and family. Things are more settled there than they may be in your practical world, which is a potential maelstrom of activity. Give yourself time to reflect on recent happenings and avoid rushing anything if at all possible. Slow and steady is the best way today.

26 SUNDAY   *Moon Age Day 8   Moon Sign Aquarius*

Romantic matters should be amiable and smooth. The closer you get to the end of the month, the more relaxed you are likely to feel, though without losing that vital 'edge'. For perhaps the first time in November thoughts of comfort, relaxation and security could be entering your mind and demanding at least some of your attention.

27 MONDAY   *Moon Age Day 9   Moon Sign Pisces*

You can continue to make the best of prevailing financial strengths and might even gain in monetary terms as a result of something you did a long time ago. Weighing up what makes those around you tick should be quite easy and you can afford to back your hunches in most matters today.

28 TUESDAY   *Moon Age Day 10   Moon Sign Pisces*

Seek out the new and unusual in life if it proves possible to do so at the moment. Anything odd or even downright weird has a specific fascination for Scorpio, and this trait is particularly emphasised at the moment. You might even be able to capitalise on this in hard financial terms if you apply your interest to objects or things which could increase in value.

29 WEDNESDAY   *Moon Age Day 11   Moon Sign Aries*

There are possible gains to be made in a monetary sense, particularly if you keep your eye on the ball and are willing to hunt out that very special bargain. Too much speculation isn't to be advised, but you should recognise a good investment when you see one. It would be hard to fool you in terms of someone's sincerity too.

30 THURSDAY   *Moon Age Day 12   Moon Sign Aries*

The strongest instinct in your life for today is to make money. Several major planets point in that direction and all of them are saying 'go on, you can do it'. To many Scorpios this will make eminent sense, so if you have been hanging back through lack of confidence, now is the time to apply yourself. Never lose sight of common sense, though.

December

2017

1 FRIDAY
Moon Age Day 13   Moon Sign Taurus

This is a day when you might have to tone down some of your recent efforts. There is no real point in pushing yourself too hard whilst the lunar low is around. To do so leads to frustration and doesn't enhance your chances of success. There are indications that you may learn something surprising about a friend.

2 SATURDAY
Moon Age Day 14   Moon Sign Taurus

Attempts to get on in life could lead to some disappointments because you are still under the influence of that rather negative Moon. Keep your expectations reasonably low and settle for a quiet time. The start of the weekend might not prove to be especially exciting, but it can lead to some unexpected gains.

3 SUNDAY
☿ *Moon Age Day 15   Moon Sign Gemini*

This is a time for capitalising on new opportunities, no matter from which direction you find them coming. Not every line of research that you follow at the moment will lead to a great revelation, though. On the contrary you may find that you will have to dig deep into life at present to get to the truth of matters.

4 MONDAY
☿ *Moon Age Day 16   Moon Sign Gemini*

The practical in life isn't quite so easy to address now as it may have been yesterday. The fact is that you are tied to certain routines that you really can't get away from. Treat these with a little respect but also find moments when you can have some fun. There are financial gains possible as the day wears on.

5 TUESDAY ☿ *Moon Age Day 17   Moon Sign Cancer*

Weigh your options carefully in the balance and don't try to proceed until you know that you are likely to succeed. This is especially important if you are a working Scorpio. Not everyone will appear to be on your side at the moment but the people who really matter should support you fully.

6 WEDNESDAY ☿ *Moon Age Day 18   Moon Sign Cancer*

You will almost certainly be drawn into the new and unusual today. Your thoughts are inspirational and you want to get on and forge new paths. There are some frustrations to be expected along the way but in the main you are frank, free and quite outspoken. Just be careful who you talk to – and the way you approach them.

7 THURSDAY ☿ *Moon Age Day 19   Moon Sign Leo*

You will actively desire to be in the public eye today and can get on very well in almost any sort of company. Practical skills come to the fore and you find yourself able to concentrate much more than has been the case of late. Certain family members bring out your grumpy side now, so stay away from them if you can.

8 FRIDAY ☿ *Moon Age Day 20   Moon Sign Leo*

You might find that outdoor interests are somehow constrained, possibly by practical developments, together with the needs that certain other people have of you. Try to save at least part of the day for doing what suits you and indulge yourself a little if you get the chance. All Scorpios need a dose of luxury now and again.

9 SATURDAY ☿ *Moon Age Day 21   Moon Sign Virgo*

Much is geared today towards practical matters and the way you view them in a moment-by-moment sense. Conforming to expected patterns is rather more difficult than it might have seemed yesterday but you can still force yourself to get on with those who have similar interests and desires. As this is the weekend, these trends are more likely to affect home than work.

10 SUNDAY ☿ *Moon Age Day 22   Moon Sign Virgo*

Beware of situations that sound too good to be true. In all probability they are. Keep your eyes wide open, particularly if there seems to be too many bargains about and use your common sense at all times. On a less practical note, do some planning now that will make the Christmas period more comfortable for everyone concerned.

11 MONDAY ☿ *Moon Age Day 23   Moon Sign Virgo*

Your curiosity tends to be powerfully stimulated today and you want to know what makes everything tick. Try to stay away from too much rich food, at least for now, because your digestive system isn't helped by present planetary positions. Family gatherings could be on the cards very soon, so be prepared.

12 TUESDAY ☿ *Moon Age Day 24   Moon Sign Libra*

This ought to be one of your better days for getting ahead in a general sense and for establishing new patterns of behaviour that are going to be useful for the future. Look at matters carefully but be prepared to act on impulse when you know instinctively that this is the right way for you to proceed.

13 WEDNESDAY ☿ *Moon Age Day 25   Moon Sign Libra*

Your ego is growing rapidly. Something you have recently done gives you cause to be proud of yourself. Don't let this fact go to your head because pride definitely does go before a fall. There are people around who need your timely advice now. Find out who they are and offer what help you can.

14 THURSDAY ☿ *Moon Age Day 26   Moon Sign Scorpio*

You are quite assertive at the moment and it would be all too easy to mislead someone as to your true opinions. So often in discussions at the moment, you will take a particular stance, simply for the sake of the argument. In your heart you know that this is never a good idea and it would be far better to tell the truth as you see it from the outset.

15 FRIDAY   ☿   *Moon Age Day 27   Moon Sign Scorpio*

Most things should fall nicely into place today and over the weekend. The lunar high supports your efforts to get everything done well ahead of Christmas week, and you manage to find time to have some real fun right now. Getting out and about would be good, as would meeting with interesting new people.

16 SATURDAY   ☿   *Moon Age Day 28   Moon Sign Scorpio*

In terms of everyday life you find it easy to adapt to the needs and wants of others. The general level of excitement should continue, and with Christmas coming there is little to prevent you from having a very good time. Although this period is not exactly inspirational, it does have plenty going for with regard to information gathering.

17 SUNDAY   ☿ *Moon Age Day 29   Moon Sign Sagittarius*

A period of security and growth begins on this Sunday, although as these trends are new in your chart, you may not recognise it today. The Sun is in your solar second house, the place it always occupies for you at this time of year. Build your dreams slowly because that way they last longer.

18 MONDAY   ☿ *Moon Age Day 0   Moon Sign Sagittarius*

A hectic pace is probably not only inevitable but also necessary today. What matters most is communication. You can talk the hind leg off a donkey, but if you can't find one of those, almost anyone will do. Even people you barely pass the time of day with as a rule are now targets for your tongue.

19 TUESDAY   ☿   *Moon Age Day 1   Moon Sign Capricorn*

Work and property matter in equal proportion today. With less of a tendency to push the social side of life, it appears that you are finally getting down to doing something concrete. Ignoring all those people who want to drag you off on their own particular form of adventure is not going to be easy, though.

20 WEDNESDAY ☿ *Moon Age Day 2   Moon Sign Capricorn*

All sorts of communications typify today. You could be on the telephone a lot, or else busy on the computer or mobile. The chances are that you are using every possible means to keep in touch with others, even with loved ones who are far away. Conforming to physical expectations could be somewhat tricky today as you are in more of a thoughtful mood.

21 THURSDAY ☿ *Moon Age Day 3   Moon Sign Capricorn*

Every Scorpio needs luxury sometimes and today is as good a time as any to get it. Although you might find it difficult to leave others to enjoy the cut and thrust of social situations, you would take well to a break from activity. The best of all worlds would be a sauna or a health spa of some sort in order fully enjoy today.

22 FRIDAY ☿ *Moon Age Day 4   Moon Sign Aquarius*

This is a time for social highlights, through business as well as family and friends. Maybe it's an office party, or some sort of gathering after work. Whatever it turns out to be you will be happy to be the life and soul of the party. Beware, though, that the same trends from earlier in the month continue, so too much eating or drinking might be a mistake.

23 SATURDAY *Moon Age Day 5   Moon Sign Aquarius*

There are entertaining experiences coming your way this weekend. It's true that you love to be in the limelight at the moment, so there is a strong possibility that half the fun in your vicinity is being created by you personally. If you are well ahead with your work, take some time out to do what pleases you.

24 SUNDAY *Moon Age Day 6   Moon Sign Pisces*

There are various ups and downs to deal with at home, though in the main you manage to maintain your sense of humour and even get up to some mischief yourself. There could be some good family news coming your way, even though you may find it to be surprising. Scorpio is very creative on this Christmas Eve.

25 MONDAY
Moon Age Day 7   Moon Sign Pisces

It is entirely likely that Christmas Day will find you in generally good spirits and able to cope with the domestic demands of the day. Most of you will be on your best behaviour and will show the naturally affectionate side of your zodiac sign. Some of the presents you receive could be howlers, but don't let that offbeat sense of humour show.

26 TUESDAY
Moon Age Day 8   Moon Sign Pisces

Boxing Day is likely to be hectic but very enjoyable. It seems you want to talk to just about anyone who comes your way and you remain cheerful and optimistic in your general state of mind. Your confidence certainly isn't lacking and you can look out for a few really unexpected surprises.

27 WEDNESDAY
Moon Age Day 9   Moon Sign Aries

You may be prone to especially high ideals or even certain illusions regarding your own life. Talk to people who are in the know and be prepared to learn from what they have to say. If you are feeling somewhat under the weather today you are likely to find that a breath of fresh air would do you good.

28 THURSDAY
Moon Age Day 10   Moon Sign Aries

The fun principle is strong for your zodiac sign as the holidays progress. Not everyone treats you as their cup of tea but that's part of the problem of being a Scorpio – most people adore you but a few people definitely don't. There isn't much point in trying too hard when the latter situation is the case.

29 FRIDAY
Moon Age Day 11   Moon Sign Taurus

On a practical level you are nowhere near as capable as you seemed to be yesterday. Don't worry because the things you can't or won't do will be dealt with by someone else. If you really feel that you have contributed everything you can to the holidays, sit back and enjoy watching everyone else work for a change.

30 SATURDAY　　　*Moon Age Day 12　Moon Sign Taurus*

You are filled with bright ideas at present. What is likely to be lacking is the necessary energy to put many of them into practice. Although you will want to make the running socially, even here you could easily run out of steam. By tomorrow, you should be getting back to normal and in the meantime you can watch life go by.

31 SUNDAY　　　*Moon Age Day 13　Moon Sign Gemini*

In a social sense it is possible that you will feel somewhat disheartened at the start of today. Scorpio people are not universally ones for New Year parties but you can get yourself into the right state of mind if you put some effort into doing so. For the sake of others, and ultimately for your own enjoyment, try to have a good time.

SCORPIO:
2018 DIARY PAGES

SCORPIO:
YOUR YEAR IN BRIEF

Stand by to get going quickly because it looks as though the start of the year is going to be quite eventful for you, as both January and February indicate forward movement and the chance to make more of yourself, both professionally and personally. This is an excellent time of good trends, so enjoy the cut and thrust of a positive and aspiring time. There is a chance that you will be starting completely new projects.

Avoid dull routines during March and April. You will get by much better if you concentrate on interesting new projects, whilst getting everyday jobs out of the way as early in each day as you can. You remain optimistic, and you will also be looking carefully at relationships and all they are offering you. This should be a lucky phase so it is therefore worth putting in that extra effort that can really count.

May and June should see you making adequate progress and you are likely to be achieving a longed-for objective, perhaps connected with travel. There is a greater likelihood of financial gains and a better sense of purpose at work, with more in the way of personal satisfaction. These trends continue during June but at this time you should be careful not to promote your own interests at the expense of others.

All trends seem to indicate that the high summer should be a really good time for you and it looks as though you will have every incentive to get on positively in most areas of your life. There are likely to be some changes at work and the possibility of long distance travel for some Scorpions. There are also likely to be new financial opportunities around during July and August and you should make as much of these as proves to be possible.

As a Scorpio the autumn is your time, and with generally good planetary trends surrounding you for most of September and October, these months should turn out to be eventful and perhaps even spectacular in one way or another. Friends could be behaving slightly oddly at this stage of the year and you might also expect some sort of relationship-based upheaval somewhere in the family. In all situations, avoid worry and take practical action.

The final months of the year, November and December, ought to see you going for gold in a number of different ways. Efforts you put in earlier now begin to pay dividends and you are on a pronounced and very important learning curve. Part of the reason you make gains at this time is because you are helping others – and learning a lot about yourself on the way. Year-end celebrations should be well marked.

January 2018

1 MONDAY
Moon Age Day 14   Moon Sign Gemini

Your mind is restless and your thoughts are like quicksilver on this New Year's Day. That's fine, as long as you use this quality wisely. There is a danger that you will spread yourself too thinly and end up achieving virtually nothing for all your efforts. At home you are likely to be constantly looking for something new to do.

2 TUESDAY
Moon Age Day 15   Moon Sign Cancer

You don't necessarily expect other people to believe everything you tell them or to agree with your point of view. That won't worry you too much because if you are sure of yourself you can remain confident that you will win through in the end. Where affairs of the heart are concerned you are very sincere now.

3 WEDNESDAY
Moon Age Day 16   Moon Sign Cancer

Try to keep thinking positively and you can have more or less what you want. All the same, keep your wishes within the bounds of sense and credibility, or you might find you are overstretching yourself. Now is a good time to come out with your own opinions, whether or not certain other people agree with them.

4 THURSDAY
Moon Age Day 17   Moon Sign Leo

Your ability to concentrate may be higher than usual. Ingenious and brilliant, you could dazzle some of the people you are in contact with at this time. Any task that requires all your attention should be tackled now, in the certain knowledge that you can complete it successfully.

5 FRIDAY
Moon Age Day 18   Moon Sign Leo

Circumstances might conspire you hold you back at first today but you need to remember just how strong your ability is right now. Don't give in when things get tough but keep going and you will push through to victory in the end. There are possible gains to be made from some unexpected directions.

6 SATURDAY
Moon Age Day 19   Moon Sign Virgo

A general feeling of wellbeing ought to attend your thoughts and actions today. If your time is your own this weekend, consider spending some of it getting involved in new projects – perhaps with groups or societies of some sort. Money matters should work out well and you might find a bargain at the shops.

7 SUNDAY
Moon Age Day 20   Moon Sign Virgo

Get out and learn new subjects if you can, while at the same time firm up your existing knowledge. It is important to be in the right place to benefit from life whilst the Sun occupies its present position and you certainly have good powers of communication. Keep up your efforts towards self-improvement.

8 MONDAY
Moon Age Day 21   Moon Sign Libra

Though today should be happy and fulfilling, you may be expected to deal with a number of different matters all at the same time. You could be rushing around from one appointment to another and failing to give situations the attention they truly deserve. Efficiency and using your time constructively is key.

9 TUESDAY
Moon Age Day 22   Moon Sign Libra

The material side of life and its little luxuries should put a smile on your face right now. Work matters have more than a few advantages attached to them and you will probably be feeling optimistic throughout most of today. Look carefully at expenditure and see if there is some way you can cut down on certain aspects of your spending.

10 WEDNESDAY   *Moon Age Day 23   Moon Sign Scorpio*

Today the Moon moves into your own zodiac sign and that means the arrival of the lunar high. You will be on top form and quite willing to take on as many challenges as possible. There are gains coming your way as a result of your own efforts but the best prizes may be the result of a little good luck.

11 THURSDAY   *Moon Age Day 24   Moon Sign Scorpio*

You should now benefit from the help that comes your way from a number of different directions. It isn't that people are any more or less co-operative than they usually are, it's just that you see things in a more positive way. Good fortune is still on your side and that means you can take a few little chances.

12 FRIDAY   *Moon Age Day 25   Moon Sign Scorpio*

If you force yourself to take things somewhat easier at this time, you should notice that you definitely get more done. There is nothing to be gained from rushing about from pillar to post so slow down and enjoy spending time on the detail. You may benefit at the moment from the good organisational skills of colleagues.

13 SATURDAY   *Moon Age Day 26   Moon Sign Sagittarius*

This ought to be a time of peace and security within the home. Matters relating to property could be uppermost in your mind and you might be quietly considering a deal that could lead to financial benefits. This would also be a good time for any sort of DIY, most particularly redecoration.

14 SUNDAY   *Moon Age Day 27   Moon Sign Sagittarius*

Appearances can be quite deceptive so check and re-check things very carefully today before you fully commit yourself to anything. There are likely to be new people coming into your life at any time and they should bring with them new interests and the chance to look at life in a slightly different way. Some excitement is close at hand.

15 MONDAY   *Moon Age Day 28*   *Moon Sign Capricorn*

You are much more likely to dig your heels in today and the co-operative, compliant soul you have been throughout much of this month is now far less evident. The thing is that you know what you want, while others see life differently. Compromise is a very good idea, but possibly one that passes you by today.

16 TUESDAY   *Moon Age Day 0*   *Moon Sign Capricorn*

The Sun is still strong in your solar chart and that makes you more of a communicator at the moment. You know what you want to say and will find new ways of putting across a message that is particularly important to you. Your social conscience is also stimulated by present planetary trends.

17 WEDNESDAY   *Moon Age Day 1*   *Moon Sign Capricorn*

What happens in everyday discussions today may be of supreme importance to your future, whether or not you realise it at the time. It is vitally important for you to listen carefully and act only after great thought. Work slowly and methodically toward the conclusion of a particular task that you have been set.

18 THURSDAY   *Moon Age Day 2*   *Moon Sign Aquarius*

Make the most of home and family, though without tying yourself to your living space too much. Despite the fact that it is the middle of winter and the weather may be bad, there are times when you need a change of space and new horizons. Get out of the house in the company of your partner or a friend and have fun.

19 FRIDAY   *Moon Age Day 3*   *Moon Sign Aquarius*

Along comes a fortunate period from a personal point of view. It seems that you will find it easy to express yourself to your partner or sweetheart and if you are not involved in a personal attachment at the moment, one could be coming along quite soon. Routines can be a chore to others today but not to you.

20 SATURDAY   *Moon Age Day 4   Moon Sign Pisces*

Comfort and security seem to mean very little to you right now and you are willing to undergo a good deal of upheaval in order to get something you really want. Once again you are capable of working hard to support others and the reforming side of your nature is very much emphasised under present trends.

21 SUNDAY   *Moon Age Day 5   Moon Sign Pisces*

It is around this time that you show what you are truly made of. Love is important and there isn't much doubt about your ability to come across as being extremely attractive. In some cases an associate or a casual friend can become much more and at the same time you have what it takes to sweep people off their feet. Scorpio is electric now.

22 MONDAY   *Moon Age Day 6   Moon Sign Pisces*

Getting your own way is now largely a matter of turning on that Scorpio charm. At the same time you appear magnetic and mysterious to some people and this makes you even more attractive than usual. The depth of your thinking is such that very few people can inhabit the world that exists within that fathomless Scorpio mind.

23 TUESDAY   *Moon Age Day 7   Moon Sign Aries*

Although you are quite practical at this stage of the week you might have to rely significantly on the good offices of others if you are going to break any records. Nevertheless you show a strong determination, which gets more obvious with every passing hour. A more potent and successful period is just around the corner.

24 WEDNESDAY   *Moon Age Day 8   Moon Sign Aries*

With the Sun presently in your solar fourth house you will spend a lot of time thinking about your family and your home surroundings. You might decide to make some sort of change that will make everyone feel more comfortable. It is likely that this will involve an investment of time rather than money.

25 THURSDAY   *Moon Age Day 9   Moon Sign Taurus*

The Moon now moves into your opposite zodiac sign of Taurus, bringing that part of the month known as the lunar low. It might be best to shelve a few tasks, at least for a day or two, while you concentrate on something you see as being of supreme importance. Better still, let others do things for you if possible.

26 FRIDAY   *Moon Age Day 10   Moon Sign Taurus*

You may be more inclined than ever to sit around and do very little today. It is unlikely that you would be depressed but you will almost certainly be feeling lazy and much less inclined than usual to push yourself. All the same, life can be quite comfortable and you can relax better than for some days.

27 SATURDAY   *Moon Age Day 11   Moon Sign Gemini*

If you have made plans to go anywhere today you might have to alter them at the last minute. This doesn't mean that you are likely to be left out in the cold or that you will have to make a cancellation. On the contrary, you have what it takes to deal with eventualities as and when they arise. Friends will automatically respond to your needs.

28 SUNDAY   *Moon Age Day 12   Moon Sign Gemini*

Make this a light-hearted time and a period during which leisure and pleasure become ever more important. There's a long way to go before you reach a particular destination that is important to you but every journey begins with the first step and that is what you are taking now. Patience works to your advantage at present.

29 MONDAY   *Moon Age Day 13   Moon Sign Cancer*

It looks as though you will be the life and soul of any party that takes place in your vicinity and you even have what it takes to organise one of your own. If there are celebrations somewhere in the family you will want to be at the heart of them and you can be especially close to either a younger or older family member now.

30 TUESDAY   *Moon Age Day 14   Moon Sign Cancer*

You continue to be fairly positive in your attitude but may not respond well to changes that are imposed upon you, especially at work. You want to make decisions for yourself and you won't be too keen to have anyone else telling you what to do. This is not at all unusual for the Scorpion, who is very independent.

31 WEDNESDAY   *Moon Age Day 15   Moon Sign Leo*

Intimate get-togethers with your loved-one are likely to be rewarding and it looks as though this might be one of the most romantic interludes since the start of the year. Any misunderstandings in deep attachments can now be addressed and resolved. You are also likely to be slightly luckier in a financial sense.

February 2018

1 THURSDAY
Moon Age Day 16   Moon Sign Leo

A change for the better is likely to come along now and chances are it is spurred off by teamwork and by general co-operation with those around you. The weather outside might not be very good but you are feeling sunny and cheerful. With plenty to do and a smile on your face most of the time it looks as though today will be fortunate.

2 FRIDAY
Moon Age Day 17   Moon Sign Virgo

It is important for you to feel connected to the past as well as the present because Scorpio dwells in both. This tendency is much enhanced at this time and you won't want to lose contact with people or situations that were formerly very important to you. All the same you can't bring back what has gone and it's pointless to try.

3 SATURDAY
Moon Age Day 18   Moon Sign Virgo

Ideas and information become central to your strategy and you can forge ahead as a result of your own efforts, whilst at the same time co-operating fully with people whose ideas conform to your own. In almost every way you now have what it takes to make significant progress although you could be over-cautious in matters of the heart.

4 SUNDAY
Moon Age Day 19   Moon Sign Libra

It is now more important than ever to recognise your roots and to connect fully with aspects of your past. At the same time you should be constantly looking forward because trends suggest that there is an issue that does need to be changed. It is also important to get onside with colleagues today.

5 MONDAY   *Moon Age Day 20   Moon Sign Libra*

You have a surplus of energy for business matters but might be slightly less inclined to socialise today. It isn't that you are not friendly but simply that you have personal issues to address. You will also be very committed to aspects of your home life and to changes you want to make to your abode.

6 TUESDAY   *Moon Age Day 21   Moon Sign Libra*

You have a naturally charming and easy-going manner under present planetary trends. You can get more or less anything you want from others at this stage though paradoxically your sensitivity to the needs and wants of those around you is not presently all that high. All you require is balance.

7 WEDNESDAY   *Moon Age Day 22   Moon Sign Scorpio*

You now reach a mental peak and will also be filled with physical energy as the Moon arrives in your own zodiac sign of Scorpio. This is the right time to take all those wonderful ideas and to make them into realities. Doing half a dozen different things at the same time ought to be quite easy, especially since everyone wants to help you.

8 THURSDAY   *Moon Age Day 23   Moon Sign Scorpio*

New ideas get the go ahead and it is almost certain that you will have energy to spare – no matter how busy you are. Because it is you who makes the running you will also make the rules and for a Scorpio that is vitally important. Although you are usually careful not to speculate too much you may be inclined to do so today.

9 FRIDAY   *Moon Age Day 24   Moon Sign Sagittarius*

Domestic and family matters are now brought into the spotlight and there is a special emphasis on property and possessions. Nostalgia will also play a significant role in your life around this time but keep your memories rooted in reality make sure that they are a true representation of what really happened.

10 SATURDAY   *Moon Age Day 25   Moon Sign Sagittarius*

Your joy for life is now much in evidence and should be able to cheer up the most miserable people and to make the whole world smile along with you. Scorpio is a pleasure to have around and you should not go short of attention whilst the Sun remains in its present position. You will become far more flexible.

11 SUNDAY   *Moon Age Day 26   Moon Sign Sagittarius*

Romantic affairs are positively highlighted and getting your own way with others across the board is simply a matter of turning on the charm and asking for what you want in the right way. Who could refuse you? If ever there was a good time to get what you want from the people around you, that time is today.

12 MONDAY   *Moon Age Day 27   Moon Sign Capricorn*

There is just a possibility you will become very slightly more withdrawn on occasions today. This has nothing to do with your enjoyment for life at the moment because that remains strong. It is simply that there are issues that can only respond to quiet thought and that will mean removing yourself from the social maelstrom for brief periods.

13 TUESDAY   *Moon Age Day 28   Moon Sign Capricorn*

Never a dull moment is the motto for today and never more so than at home. You seem to be in a most enjoyable phase for your personal life and you should be enjoying all the benefits that love and romance have to offer. Don't get tied up with tedious rules and regulations that do not apply to you.

14 WEDNESDAY   *Moon Age Day 29   Moon Sign Aquarius*

The need to feel busy and useful is paramount, even if that means clearing up after others and sorting out situations that have nothing to do with you. Some of the things you hear other people say are clearly out of kilter with what you know to be the truth but it might be best for the moment to bite your tongue.

15 THURSDAY   *Moon Age Day 0   Moon Sign Aquarius*

Prepare for a pleasant spell at home and a comfortable day during which you will not be taking on too many pressures. That's fine as far as it goes but some Scorpios will miss the cut and thrust of the action and some of you might even resort to looking for issues or problems just so you can react!

16 FRIDAY   *Moon Age Day 1   Moon Sign Aquarius*

Dealings with superiors or people in authority might prove to be a little awkward or troublesome during the last part of this working week and you will need to be as patient as possible if you are to avoid losing your temper. Better by far to simply walk away from trouble rather than reacting to it.

17 SATURDAY   *Moon Age Day 2   Moon Sign Pisces*

Strong opinions are something you cannot avoid at the moment and you are inclined to speak your mind, even when to do so could be against your best interests. It's a good thing therefore that others respect your honesty and it is unlikely that anyone would discriminate against you just because you care.

18 SUNDAY   *Moon Age Day 3   Moon Sign Pisces*

Maximise your potential by paying attention. Nobody concentrates more or for longer than you and this is a factor that will see you winning through in the end. While others look for short-term gains your mind is cast way ahead, perhaps even years into the future – but you can also do yourself a lot of good right now.

19 MONDAY   *Moon Age Day 4   Moon Sign Aries*

You continue to be quite positive and even a little dominant right now, so much so that some people will marvel at your staying power and tenacity. This is not a Monday during which you should be retreating into the background. When the opportunity comes along to shine in a public setting to turn the switch up to full.

20 TUESDAY
Moon Age Day 5   Moon Sign Aries

What loved ones have to offer today should be doubly reassuring and can have a marked bearing on the way you are thinking about life generally. You will be happy to go along with family plans and won't be in the mood to argue over details you now see as being of no real importance. The same may not be true for at least one person, though.

21 WEDNESDAY
Moon Age Day 6   Moon Sign Taurus

What you get from this midweek period is very much down to the way you approach situations. It is important not to pit yourself against challenges that are never going to work out for you no matter how much you try. Keep your expectations simple and enjoy what life offers naturally. If you are sensible, happiness prevails.

22 THURSDAY
Moon Age Day 7   Moon Sign Taurus

Don't jump to negative conclusions today and rest easy in the knowledge that there is assistance around if you need it. Take a measured view of situations and enjoy what your home life and personal relationships have to offer. This is not a good time for gambling or for taking any risks or chances.

23 FRIDAY
Moon Age Day 8   Moon Sign Taurus

Relationships are strong but you could falter slightly at work – most likely because of circumstances that are beyond your immediate control. In the main the most significant aspect of today is that it makes you quieter and less inclined to speak your mind. You will have to rely more heavily on others.

24 SATURDAY
Moon Age Day 9   Moon Sign Gemini

Don't be put off today just because not everything appears to be going your way. Some inventive thinking is necessary and at the same time you should find moments that are filled with nothing but personal happiness. Try to be less of a social reformer for a few hours and relax in good company.

25 SUNDAY   *Moon Age Day 10   Moon Sign Gemini*

Though your practical abilities are considerable at the moment you may stumble a little if you are expected to speak in any public arena. This is not because you have any doubt about your subject but merely because you doubt yourself. Your confidence is likely to grow as the day advances.

26 MONDAY   *Moon Age Day 11   Moon Sign Cancer*

This is going to be a day during which you can contribute heavily to your own success in love and relationships generally. Your magnetic and electric personality is especially attractive to others at the moment and you won't have any difficulty impressing anyone. Routines will seem a chore so ignore them altogether if you can.

27 TUESDAY   *Moon Age Day 12   Moon Sign Cancer*

In a dynamic mood, you are very good to know. Not everyone you meet will be on the same wavelength, so pick your companions today carefully. It is towards the odd or the unusual that your mind is likely to turn at the moment and you see benefits and positive advantages in some unlikely places.

28 WEDNESDAY   *Moon Age Day 13   Moon Sign Leo*

Today should be especially interesting in terms of romance. Perhaps it's the arrival of the spring or it could simply be the present position of Venus in your solar chart. Whatever the reason, you are anxious to prove just how loving and loveable you can be. Even the most unlikely people respond to your present warmth.

March

2018

1 THURSDAY   *Moon Age Day 14   Moon Sign Leo*

Your partner is now likely to do all he or she can to make you feel better about yourself and to safeguard your best interests. You should be feeling loved and protected from a number of different directions though there is a small chance that you could feel slightly suffocated by all this attention and care.

2 FRIDAY   *Moon Age Day 15   Moon Sign Virgo*

There could be some unappealing jobs to be tackled today, and it would be very useful if you could somehow delegate a few of them. Since your powers of persuasion are now so good you could make a virtue of fooling others into thinking you are doing them a favour when it is really the other way round.

3 SATURDAY   *Moon Age Day 16   Moon Sign Virgo*

Although you are likely to be in a reflective mood today there is no reason why you should avoid either thinking big or putting plans into action. When you need assistance it should be close at hand, although you will mostly be happy to go it alone. In matters of the heart you will be dominant but attractive.

4 SUNDAY   *Moon Age Day 17   Moon Sign Libra*

Communication, meeting people and getting on with what seems most important – that's the way your day is likely to go. The really important thing is to get your ideas across in a way that enchants others and convinces them to get on board with you. This is certainly no time to be shrinking violet or to doubt your own abilities.

5 MONDAY
Moon Age Day 18   Moon Sign Libra

With the Sun still in your solar fifth house you are effervescent and extremely creative. Getting things looking right should be quite easy and you also have what it takes to please the sensitivities of those close to you. Romance is well highlighted in your chart and you tend to turn heads wherever you go at this stage of the month.

6 TUESDAY
Moon Age Day 19   Moon Sign Scorpio

This ought to be a very good day when it comes to calling the shots and such is your confidence at this time that few people would deny you the right to make the running. Your personal influence across the board is likely to be strong and you positively make things happen. The world can be your oyster!

7 WEDNESDAY
Moon Age Day 20   Moon Sign Scorpio

Some of your dreams are getting bigger than they used to be but you sense that you are not overplaying your hand. If you can conceive it at the moment you can probably also put it into action, which is why it is so important to remain positive. Good fortune is yours for the taking – so just take it.

8 THURSDAY
Moon Age Day 21   Moon Sign Sagittarius

You are able to express yourself extremely well at this stage of the month and that can be very important when it comes to progressing in life generally. Money matters should be easy to deal with but you may need to curb the spending tendencies of family members, some of whom think your funds are bottomless.

9 FRIDAY
Moon Age Day 22   Moon Sign Sagittarius

There is something quite dramatic about you now and in a sense you have lost your way because you should be on the stage. You can turn almost anything into a wonderful story and that is one of the reasons why you get on so well with others at this time. Socially, people find you to be eminently reasonable.

10 SATURDAY   *Moon Age Day 23   Moon Sign Sagittarius*

Your increasing self-confidence lands you in a positive social scene. Avoid getting involved in complicated situations with friends and don't be drawn into disputes or arguments that have nothing to do with you. At home you should be feeling extremely kind and loving, which people appreciate.

11 SUNDAY   *Moon Age Day 24   Moon Sign Capricorn*

Others seem to take an opposite view to you on many different occasions today and a degree of patience is called for if you are not to lose your temper at some stage. You could also be subject to a number of delays or cancellations, all of which conspire to leave you feeling slightly frustrated and somewhat impotent in one way or another.

12 MONDAY   *Moon Age Day 25   Moon Sign Capricorn*

Your professional life now needs a narrower focus and you can't afford to spread your talents about too much under present trends. It would be far better to do one thing properly than a wealth of tasks badly. Trends indicate that the start of this working week may also coincide with a memorable social event.

13 TUESDAY   *Moon Age Day 26   Moon Sign Aquarius*

Regular and social activities are what count today and though you may not be doing much that is out of the ordinary you can turn mundane situations into little adventures. Try things differently and get others involved in your life to a greater extent. Enjoy what romance has to offer you at this most fortunate time.

14 WEDNESDAY   *Moon Age Day 27   Moon Sign Aquarius*

Your concern now turns in the direction of orderliness and efficiency. You will find it difficult to understand people who are messy or unprepared and you will tend to favour those who have a similar attitude to life. Plan for the short-term rather than looking too far ahead and make the most of little opportunities that come your way.

15 THURSDAY   *Moon Age Day 28   Moon Sign Aquarius*

Now you have the chance to improve your popularity rating, even amongst people you haven't always seen eye-to-eye with in the past. Those who may have seen you as being somewhat too dominant before are now more likely to understand your motivations and will be inclined to judge you less harshly in the future.

16 FRIDAY   *Moon Age Day 29   Moon Sign Pisces*

You should be able to capitalise on advantages at work and will be doing everything you can to get ahead financially at the moment. However, you should not worry about cash to the exclusion of everything else because some of the most important gifts that come to you at the moment do not carry any sort of price tag.

17 SATURDAY   *Moon Age Day 0   Moon Sign Pisces*

Make an early start with all tasks and duties – that way you will leave yourself more time later for personal enjoyment. There should be plenty happening that will captivate your imagination and some interesting people may also emerge. Don't get tied down with pointless rules and regulations today.

18 SUNDAY   *Moon Age Day 1   Moon Sign Aries*

Someone you don't see too often is likely to make an appearance around now and could bring with them memories of the past that are strong and emotional. Today offers all sorts of practical opportunities but it is just possible that you will fail to address some of these if your mind is too closely focused on things that happened years ago.

19 MONDAY   *Moon Age Day 2   Moon Sign Aries*

Certain matters could come to a head in professional situations and you would be well advised to keep your wits about you when at work. Respond quickly and positively to changing circumstances and don't leave anything to chance. You like to take command, even if you do so quietly and without fuss.

20 TUESDAY   *Moon Age Day 3   Moon Sign Aries*

Opportunities for excitement are on the way and at least some of them have to do with movement in your life generally. If there are journeys on offer you should grab such chances as confidently and quickly as you can. Get firmly behind a friend who is coming up with a notion you see as being both honourable and potentially rewarding.

21 WEDNESDAY   *Moon Age Day 4   Moon Sign Taurus*

Don't decide to do anything crucial today and keep to tried and tested paths. The lunar low always seems more severe when you have been moving along at a fast pace and that has certainly been the case for you. It's a little like having the brakes applied and you will need to put in masses of extra effort today if you want to keep advancing.

22 THURSDAY   *Moon Age Day 5   Moon Sign Taurus*

Energy could be in short supply and today may come as a welcome break from all the activity that has been surrounding you of late. Family members will be both funny and entertaining and it is in their direction that you are most likely to turn at this time. Despite the lunar low you should be happy to join in with the fun.

23 FRIDAY   ☿   *Moon Age Day 6   Moon Sign Gemini*

Work and practical matters are once again on the up and the position of the Sun at this time is the reason. If fresh job offers are presented you should be quite willing to look at these positively. There are gains to be made within personal relationships and once again the light of love is in your eyes. Be available to help you partner today.

24 SATURDAY   ☿   *Moon Age Day 7   Moon Sign Gemini*

The atmosphere in your life generally could perhaps best be described as one of anticipation. There is plenty that you want to do, and many opportunities that seem to be on offer – yet the time is not quite right to act. Curb your impatience this weekend by finding something to do that is enjoyable and which pleases your partner.

25 SUNDAY ☿ *Moon Age Day 8* *Moon Sign Cancer*

The means to build on recent successes is all around you but it takes a very original view of life to fully appreciate this. In some ways you are quite ingenious at the moment and will often use unconventional means in order to get your way. Friends should prove to be helpful and amenable to your suggestions.

26 MONDAY ☿ *Moon Age Day 9* *Moon Sign Cancer*

It's true that you might have to put in extra hours this week at work but the progress you will make as a result shows that the effort is well worthwhile. It is towards the material side of life that your mind now turns and you may find that you are not interested in socialising until the middle of the week.

27 TUESDAY ☿ *Moon Age Day 10* *Moon Sign Leo*

It is towards the very practical aspects of life that your mind is turning and there is plenty of assistance around at the moment if you choose to call on it. You might not be quite as tolerant of others as would sometimes be the case and this is definitely true when you are dealing with people who you feel simply won't use any common sense.

28 WEDNESDAY ☿ *Moon Age Day 11* *Moon Sign Leo*

Get together with friends and discover new ways to have fun. You should also make the most of the time of year because it should be more than obvious to you now that the worst of winter is finished and the spring is poised to lighten your life. Some of the darkness at the heart of the Scorpio nature is now blown away.

29 THURSDAY ☿ *Moon Age Day 12* *Moon Sign Virgo*

You are forceful and determined but take care to move with just a little caution, especially when you are dealing with people who are hesitant or nervy by nature. Not everyone has either your fortitude or your conviction and your absolute certainty could scare a colleague or friend.

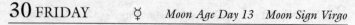

30 FRIDAY   ☿   *Moon Age Day 13   Moon Sign Virgo*

You have what it takes to make the tide of fortune flow in your direction and you do this without any tangible effort. Practical common sense makes it easy for you to steer a path between potential obstacles, while your charm means that no one can refuse any reasonable request. Money matters should be solid.

31 SATURDAY   ☿   *Moon Age Day 14   Moon Sign Libra*

A little peace and quiet – which in some ways appears to be quite inviting, simply isn't going to be possible under present trends. On the contrary, you are in demand from both family members and friends. Trying to find moments to please yourself might mean having to disappoint someone – and you don't want that.

April
2018

1 SUNDAY
☿ *Moon Age Day 15   Moon Sign Libra*

There could be fewer advantages on the professional scene at the start of this month. Life can seem quite complicated and you will have to work extra hard in order to get the simplest things done. Socially, things should be significantly more successful and you have what it takes to make friends and influence people.

2 MONDAY
☿ *Moon Age Day 16   Moon Sign Scorpio*

Now is the time to take many of your previous plans and make them into realities. There are gains coming along that you may not have foreseen – though most of these are as a result of your past efforts. Good luck follows you around and this is a period during which you can afford to take more chances than usual.

3 TUESDAY
☿ *Moon Age Day 17   Moon Sign Scorpio*

Put fresh ideas to the test and make suggestions to see how others react. Your powers of persuasion are now especially good and it won't be hard for you to get your own way, often without others realising that it is happening. Instigate as much change as possible in your life, and take the chance to travel if possible.

4 WEDNESDAY
☿ *Moon Age Day 18   Moon Sign Scorpio*

You are productive at work and should be doing especially well if you are involved in any sort of educational process at the moment. As is often the case for Scorpio you will also delight in catering for the needs of others. This is especially the case for Scorpios who are involved in the caring professions.

5 THURSDAY ☿ *Moon Age Day 19* *Moon Sign Sagittarius*

You could find yourself thrown into opposing positions on a number of occasions today. One thing that is certain about Scorpios is that they stick to their guns and it is very unlikely that you will change your mind about anything just to please the crowd. In the end, people warm to you because of your convictions.

6 FRIDAY ☿ *Moon Age Day 20* *Moon Sign Sagittarius*

You can bring out the good side of all those you encounter today. There is a strong chance you will feel especially warm towards certain individuals – even some you haven't cared for much in the past. Your communication skills are very good at the moment and you can do yourself no end of good if you just keep on talking.

7 SATURDAY ☿ *Moon Age Day 21* *Moon Sign Capricorn*

Practical matters are highlighted today and you will be right on the ball when it comes to getting yourself organised. At the same time you are likely to be looking quite earnestly at the romantic side of your life and inventing new ways to pep things up a little. Some of your more practical plans should now be moving towards completion.

8 SUNDAY ☿ *Moon Age Day 22* *Moon Sign Capricorn*

Prepare for some unavoidable changes now. Although you may not at first welcome these, try to adapt and you should soon see the benefits in the changing circumstances. Intellectually, you are clearly on the ball and your quick mind should make short work of puzzles or downright mysteries.

9 MONDAY ☿ *Moon Age Day 23* *Moon Sign Capricorn*

Things taking place at work, or within social groups of which you are a part make it possible for you to be progressive and even excited at prospects that stand before you. There is something unusual about your mood at this time and you are extremely innovative and even pioneering in a number of ways.

10 TUESDAY ☿ *Moon Age Day 24   Moon Sign Aquarius*

The greatest rewards are still likely to come from personal relationships and fortunate encounters with people you really like. Don't expect all the compliments today to come from the direction you would normally think most likely and be prepared to be flavour of the month with at least one very surprising individual.

11 WEDNESDAY ☿ *Moon Age Day 25   Moon Sign Aquarius*

All group encounters are likely to work well for you and this is a time when you should be quite happy to co-operate fully with others. This could be with friends or colleagues but whatever the circumstances might be, you will quite happily forego your own personal opinions for the sake of cordiality.

12 THURSDAY ☿ *Moon Age Day 26   Moon Sign Pisces*

Real fulfilment today comes when you give up all thought of standing out from the crowd and throw in your lot with those around you. The greater the co-operation, the better the results and you can feel warm inside at the thought of your contribution to communal efforts. In quiet moments you should also be quite contemplative now.

13 FRIDAY ☿ *Moon Age Day 27   Moon Sign Pisces*

Avoid getting on the wrong side of people in authority. They probably won't mind too much if you disagree with them but you may worry and fret about the situation later. There is no reason to fall out with anyone at this time; that is unless you allow the really stubborn side of your nature to predominate.

14 SATURDAY ☿ *Moon Age Day 28   Moon Sign Pisces*

What a good period this can be for communications amongst your friends. You take an important role of new plans that are being laid down and there is also a chance you will be organising a journey you intend to make in the not too distant future. In a physical sense you should remain active and will be a winner.

15 SUNDAY   *Moon Age Day 29   Moon Sign Aries*

There ought to be plenty going on as far as your domestic life is concerned, even if things are slowing down a little in other areas. Keep abreast of local news and views and perhaps consider getting involved in an important community project. This is a good time to plan ahead.

16 MONDAY   *Moon Age Day 0   Moon Sign Aries*

Intimate relationships could prove to be rather demanding this week and you will need to ring the changes a little and to get away from the intensity by concentrating on casual friendships too. Scorpio tends to smoulder in an emotional sense and there are times when a lighter touch works its own magic.

17 TUESDAY   *Moon Age Day 1   Moon Sign Taurus*

Stand by for a few complications – that is unless you are very organised. The lunar low is inclined to make you see things in a rather peculiar way and it is unlikely that you will find all the answers you seek until later in the week. For today, allow colleagues and friends to take most of the strain.

18 WEDNESDAY   *Moon Age Day 2   Moon Sign Taurus*

There are still likely to be some setbacks to deal with but as far as relationships are concerned everything should be plain sailing. You will instinctively realise this and are likely to be staying close to home if you possibly can. Something you are positively yearning for will just have to wait for a while.

19 THURSDAY   *Moon Age Day 3   Moon Sign Gemini*

Independent efforts are not half so productive at the moment as co-operative ventures. This is partly because of planetary trends but also on account of your need for reassurance and support. To others you often seem to be overflowing with confidence and quite able to stand alone but at its core Scorpio is rarely as positive as it looks.

20 FRIDAY   *Moon Age Day 4   Moon Sign Gemini*

You show are warm-hearted and soft with family members but you will also be just as attentive to strangers. This is the kind side of Scorpio and is particularly obvious at the moment because your social-reforming impulses are much aroused. You want to help anyone who is less well off or confident than you presently are.

21 SATURDAY   *Moon Age Day 5   Moon Sign Cancer*

Personal relationships look especially good on this April Saturday and it appears you have what it takes to make the best possible impression on people who have only recently come into your life. Your sporting instincts are aroused and you have a strong competitive edge that may assure you of victory.

22 SUNDAY   *Moon Age Day 6   Moon Sign Cancer*

Your romantic feelings towards others are definitely on the increase so this might turn out to be one of the most interesting parts of April as far as intimate attachments are concerned. Scorpio simmers with emotion and you can also find the right words to make that most important person love you all the more. Protect your financial interests.

23 MONDAY   *Moon Age Day 7   Moon Sign Leo*

Relationships continue to bring out the best in you and although you still have a great desire to get on in a material sense it is towards your personal life that you turn more and more. However, this will not prevent you from looking and planning ahead, especially where travel is concerned. You now have what it takes to invest wisely.

24 TUESDAY   *Moon Age Day 8   Moon Sign Leo*

Your ability to get to the core of the thought processes of your relatives and friends is almost uncanny today. You are especially aware of opportunities to make progress in a material sense but will also be quite busy organising the lives of people who really need your special touch. In some ways, today could be exhausting but also rewarding.

25 WEDNESDAY *Moon Age Day 9   Moon Sign Virgo*

Meetings with colleagues and friends should now be free from any sort of complications and life is just about as simple as it can be. This is especially good for Scorpio, which always seems to be in the midst of one intrigue or another. For once, you are not interested in secrets – either your own or those of people around you.

26 THURSDAY *Moon Age Day 10   Moon Sign Virgo*

The sense of responsibility you feel towards others could easily get in the way of your own desires today but as is usually the case for Scorpio, duty comes first. It would be very wise to seek the help and support of people who have particular skills and to realise that you can't solve all the problems yourself.

27 FRIDAY *Moon Age Day 11   Moon Sign Virgo*

Intimacy with a loved one transcends usual boundaries and it looks as though you can achieve a connection that often escapes you. This is because you are less locked inside your own deep nature. You show freshness and a natural vitality that is very attractive to others. In a professional sense you should be on a roll at the moment.

28 SATURDAY *Moon Age Day 12   Moon Sign Libra*

Subtle changes in the nature of events can make your goals and objectives less certain at the moment. That is why it would be best to pause and take stock of matters. There isn't much point in ploughing on regardless because this will result in you having to do things again. Friends should be very supportive.

29 SUNDAY *Moon Age Day 13   Moon Sign Libra*

Old patterns of thinking break down slightly and you could stumble a little under the weight of responsibility. Some of these are far less onerous than you think and in any case there is help and support around if you look for it. Someone you haven't seen for ages could be making a return to your life.

30 MONDAY · *Moon Age Day 14 · Moon Sign Scorpio*

With the lunar high comes a period during which you can afford to take a few more risks than has been possible for a short while. You seem to be getting ahead without trying too hard, which leaves time and incentive for new ideas and revised strategies. Almost everyone you come across at the moment has your best interests at heart.

May

2018

1 TUESDAY
Moon Age Day 15   Moon Sign Scorpio

Eliminate old convictions and turn your mind to the future with less inclination to hang on to the past. Scorpio is famous for maintaining a way of being that is sometimes distinctly old fashioned but this is much less likely under present trends. On the contrary you are about as contemporary as it is possible to be.

2 WEDNESDAY
Moon Age Day 16   Moon Sign Sagittarius

People you meet around this time may offer some good advice and you would be well advised to listen carefully to it. Taken together with your own slant on life their considerations can help you make a greater success of present efforts. This is certainly no time to go it alone or to be churlish about co-operation.

3 THURSDAY
Moon Age Day 17   Moon Sign Sagittarius

You should now be fully abreast of all that is taking place in the world around you and very little will avoid your scrutiny under present planetary trends. Being so much on the ball you won't be easily fooled but the same is not true for your friends, some of whom really do need your wise counsel and sound advice at this time.

4 FRIDAY
Moon Age Day 18   Moon Sign Sagittarius

Look for a special time with someone you love and make this a day for showing how deep your affections run. In the midst of a busy life it is sometimes difficult to find the time you need to say the right things and to offer undying support but that isn't the case now. There ought to be plenty of moments to prove your devotion.

5 SATURDAY
Moon Age Day 19   Moon Sign Capricorn

Look for intimacy and make a big fuss of your partner. This is the person you rely on the most and they deserve your unswerving loyalty and assistance when it is needed. Outside of romance you could be making important new friends and might even meet someone you wish you had known for most of your life. This is a good day to smile.

6 SUNDAY
Moon Age Day 20   Moon Sign Capricorn

You should be feeling very warm and affectionate whilst the Sun is in your solar seventh house and you could also be on the receiving end of romantic gestures. Whether all of these come from an accepted or even an acceptable direction remains to be seen but you ought to be quite flattered in by the attention.

7 MONDAY
Moon Age Day 21   Moon Sign Aquarius

This should be a wonderful time for intimate encounters and for strengthening the ties between yourself and your life partner. If you don't have a life partner and wish you did, now is a really good time to be looking around. Sometimes things are more likely to come your way if you put in the right sort of effort at an opportune moment.

8 TUESDAY
Moon Age Day 22   Moon Sign Aquarius

It's time to seek wide-open spaces and to make the most of the natural world that surrounds you. With the early summer comes a greater desire to encounter nature in all its variety and you will now be much more inclined to spend time out of doors. This would also be a great time to take an early holiday.

9 WEDNESDAY
Moon Age Day 23   Moon Sign Aquarius

Some key aims and objectives are due for an overhaul and you will be putting your mind to the test on a very regular basis. Not everything is going to go your way first time and there is merit in trying again when something does go wrong. As far as using up your time is concerned try to strike a sensible balance between work and home.

10 THURSDAY   *Moon Age Day 24   Moon Sign Pisces*

Chats and even debates with others should prove inspirational and can be the source of many new ideas. Open-minded and active, you have what it takes to be out there succeeding for most of the time. Keep a sense of proportion when it comes to looking after your money and rein in your spending.

11 FRIDAY   *Moon Age Day 25   Moon Sign Pisces*

Strength of will is one of your greatest virtues, as is the ability to keep going when others have fallen by the wayside. You will not only be sorting out your own life around now but also spending time making sure that everyone else is getting what they desire. In reality it's easier to help others now than to help yourself.

12 SATURDAY   *Moon Age Day 26   Moon Sign Aries*

You could probably benefit from the advice of someone who is older or wiser than you are and when it comes to certain tasks you might have to call on the support of professionals. Your home environment is likely to prove very supportive and you can make the most of all the positive influences brought to your life by friends.

13 SUNDAY   *Moon Age Day 27   Moon Sign Aries*

When it comes to professional matters you are now likely to adopt a more rugged approach and you won't suffer fools gladly. The chances are you will do everything you can for people who are willing to help themselves but you will fight shy of giving constant assistance when you know it is wasted. Look forward to a good social evening.

14 MONDAY   *Moon Age Day 28   Moon Sign Taurus*

There is a slight chance you will feel somewhat alone and probably slightly confused whilst the lunar low is around this month. You may not receive the degree of support that you feel you need, though if you look at situations without emotion you will soon see that nothing is expected of you that you haven't done a thousand times before.

15 TUESDAY
Moon Age Day 0   Moon Sign Taurus

Taking risks is probably not a sensible option for today at least. Once again it is important to stick to what you know and understand, whilst staying away from anything that might get you into trouble or which could prove physically dangerous. You would prefer to feel safe and secure, and probably to be at home too.

16 WEDNESDAY
Moon Age Day 1   Moon Sign Gemini

Certain desires can now be met more successfully than would have been the case on Monday or Tuesday but it could take you a few hours today to get up to speed. In particular you seem to be doing well in all co-operative ventures and where your unique and sometimes off-the-wall ideas are valued.

17 THURSDAY
Moon Age Day 2   Moon Sign Gemini

Your intuition is fairly strong, except when you are dealing with matters that have a bearing on your own personal or romantic life. When it comes to assessing others and situations beyond your own life you will be excellent. Don't be surprised if people naturally turn to you for help and advice today and be ready to do what you can.

18 FRIDAY
Moon Age Day 3   Moon Sign Cancer

You should find plenty of contentment today if you spend as much time as possible with friends. Don't do anything particularly unusual but stick to what you know and like. There should be opportunities to move around a good deal and any sort of journey, whether it has been planned for weeks or not, would benefit you.

19 SATURDAY
Moon Age Day 4   Moon Sign Cancer

Some matters could prove to be quite tiresome today and you certainly won't want to talk for hours on end to people who seem to have nothing sensible to say. In addition it could seem that you are spending valuable hours doing things you know are a waste of time. In this regard at least, a rethink might be in order later in the day.

20 SUNDAY
Moon Age Day 5   Moon Sign Leo

There are small gains to be made today, and although none of these seem especially important in themselves they could begin to add up as the day wears on. Attitude is very important when it comes to a professional offer that might be on the table. This could be a sideways move of some sort but it may have its benefits.

21 MONDAY
Moon Age Day 6   Moon Sign Leo

Stand by for a fairly productive period as far as money is concerned. It isn't that there is more cash about than you might expect but more that you are using what you have more effectively. Attention to detail is very important when you are at work and it is essential that get things right first time every time.

22 TUESDAY
Moon Age Day 7   Moon Sign Leo

Travel generally seems to be especially important at the moment and today ought to offer you quite a few opportunities to do something different. Part of you wants to follow the same old routines but you need to realise that change and diversity are essential as well. Friends can seem rather pushy.

23 WEDNESDAY
Moon Age Day 8   Moon Sign Virgo

You come across to others as being tremendously sociable and especially charming for most of the rest of this week. This means you are in an ideal position to chase something you have wanted for ages. Those people who are in a position to do you some good are looking at you in a very positive way right now.

24 THURSDAY
Moon Age Day 9   Moon Sign Virgo

There should now be a significant opportunity to get a backlog of work cleared up – even if you have to bully others into helping you. There are gains to be made on the financial front, mainly because your organisational skills are so good, but you should also be on the receiving end of some significant luck at present.

25 FRIDAY $\qquad$ *Moon Age Day 10   Moon Sign Libra*

You are now inclined to act on impulse and will leave behind that less-than-positive and suspicious quality that lies at the heart of Scorpio. You should be physically active at the moment and won't be held back by the sort of situation that sometimes hampers you. On the contrary you will positively welcome most challenges.

26 SATURDAY $\qquad$ *Moon Age Day 11   Moon Sign Libra*

A period of significant change is now upon you and this is likely to mean 'out with the old and in with the new'. Although planetary trends are good you won't always want to part with certain aspects of the past, if only because of your nostalgic turn of mind. Be ruthless and ditch any emotional baggage.

27 SUNDAY $\qquad$ *Moon Age Day 12   Moon Sign Scorpio*

There is genuine power at your fingertips and you will be happy to have a go at almost anything now that the lunar high has arrived. This is the time of the month to throw caution to the wind and to go out and get what you want the most. Getting others to follow your lead should be easy and the admirers are gathering.

28 MONDAY $\qquad$ *Moon Age Day 13   Moon Sign Scorpio*

Your energy levels are increasing and you may benefit from a little good luck. This would be a great day for a shopping spree or for doing something completely different alongside those you find stimulating and fascinating. If you have to cross swords with anyone at the moment you will find yourself winning the argument without really trying.

29 TUESDAY $\qquad$ *Moon Age Day 14   Moon Sign Sagittarius*

Conversations with your partner or sweetheart may well be on the cards today. Leave these until you have sufficient time to talk at length and don't crowd your schedule today with all sorts of tasks that have no real significance. You might have to be discriminating at work and this could mean disappointing someone.

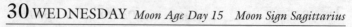

30 WEDNESDAY *Moon Age Day 15   Moon Sign Sagittarius*

Your chart for today indicates that you should trust someone. Scorpio is usually inclined to be rather sceptical and rarely considers that anyone does anything other than for selfless reasons. Suspicion is the hallmark of your zodiac sign but it might be slightly too prevalent under present planetary trends.

31 THURSDAY *Moon Age Day 16   Moon Sign Sagittarius*

You can widen your horizons under present trends and should get on especially well with people who are naturally optimistic and dynamic. Leave alone those individuals whose presence in your life is a drain on your physical and mental resources. You may need to be firm with a wayward family member.

June

2018

1 FRIDAY
Moon Age Day 17   Moon Sign Capricorn

You tend to be very focused at the present time so if there is anything you need to organise this is clearly the best time to do it. Some of your career goals could be uppermost in your mind and it should be easy for you to persuade others to agree with even audacious plans. You should be on top form physically.

2 SATURDAY
Moon Age Day 18   Moon Sign Capricorn

Keep up your efforts to forge ahead because although the weekend might mean there is little progress to be made as far as work is concerned your mind is clearly working overtime and you see your way ahead all too clearly. Also have some fun today and spend as many hours as possible with loved ones.

3 SUNDAY
Moon Age Day 19   Moon Sign Aquarius

In joint financial affairs there is likely to be more in the way of good fortune coming your way. Co-operation now seems to be the key to success and you should be more than happy to throw in your lot with people who know where they are going. There could be the odd delay or difficulty but nothing you can't deal with.

4 MONDAY
Moon Age Day 20   Moon Sign Aquarius

Travel could now be uppermost in your mind and it looks as though Scorpio is getting itchy feet. You may simply be taking journeys in your locality but for a few lucky ones amongst you the world beckons. What is most important around now is to avoid getting stuck in any sort of rut, either socially or with regard to your home life.

5 TUESDAY   *Moon Age Day 21   Moon Sign Aquarius*

You can capitalise on new opportunities in the professional world and some Scorpions will now be on the receiving end of offers that mean more responsibility but also better financial remuneration. You tend to be looking after your personal resources very carefully and you won't spend too much on pointless luxuries.

6 WEDNESDAY   *Moon Age Day 22   Moon Sign Pisces*

An ability to win the confidence of your friends is inherent in your nature but there are so many awkward people around at the moment that it could be quite difficult to do so. In the case of one particular task it is likely that the hard work has already been done and you can afford to slacken your pace. Make the most of strong social trends.

7 THURSDAY   *Moon Age Day 23   Moon Sign Pisces*

You could be quite contemplative but at the same time you know how important it will be to make a good impression on the right people. This could be almost anyone from a really important person in authority figure to someone you have never met before. Class or standing doesn't really come into it today because you are interested in everyone.

8 FRIDAY   *Moon Age Day 24   Moon Sign Aries*

At work you have the ability to create a good impression. This can be quite important because there are gains to be made and people to influence. This word 'influence' is very important to Scorpio this year, especially so at this time. You know that life is not a rehearsal and so you do all you can to get to the winning post early.

9 SATURDAY   *Moon Age Day 25   Moon Sign Aries*

You need the freedom to go out and make the right sort of discoveries – things that are going to be of importance to you in the weeks and months ahead. With a better understanding of what is needed in any given situation you won't fail to impress the right people and should create a weekend fit to remember.

10 SUNDAY   *Moon Age Day 26   Moon Sign Aries*

Independence is valued highly by Scorpio at the best of times but proves to be extremely important under present trends. You certainly won't take at all kindly to being told what to do by people you cannot admire and if you are put into uncomfortable situations it is quite likely that you will speak out.

11 MONDAY   *Moon Age Day 27   Moon Sign Taurus*

Things should quieten down whilst the lunar low is in evidence but this period will at least give you the chance to formalise your plans for the future and you are unlikely to be bothered by outside influences to the extent that has been the case recently. Withdrawing into your own little world does have its own advantages.

12 TUESDAY   *Moon Age Day 28   Moon Sign Taurus*

This is definitely the right time of the month to recharge your batteries. Let others do things for you and don't be too worried if some jobs are being put on hold. You are unlikely to feel too anxious about responsibilities because in most respects you are well on top of things, which is probably why you are so willing to take a break.

13 WEDNESDAY   *Moon Age Day 0   Moon Sign Gemini*

A greater sense of freedom also brings the desire to look at the world in more detail – which probably means travel. If you have a holiday planned for this period you have chosen wisely, but even if you can only find the time to go to the shops or the local park you can still learn something of importance.

14 THURSDAY   *Moon Age Day 1   Moon Sign Gemini*

It looks as though you are in the mood for romance and what you learn from others makes you even more inclined to be the perfect suitor. Let your light shine in social situations and be prepared to be the life and soul of any party that is taking place. If there isn't one in the offing you may need to arrange it for yourself.

15 FRIDAY   *Moon Age Day 2   Moon Sign Cancer*

Keep your eyes and ears open for new input at this time and enjoy the cut and thrust of a fairly hectic life. Get ahead of yourself by doing something that doesn't really need to be completed for a while and be prepared to do a little extra at home in order to free yourself from routines in the days that lie ahead.

16 SATURDAY   *Moon Age Day 3   Moon Sign Cancer*

There is more than enough pressure in your life to be going on with for the moment. Try to be bold in your strategies but also check details before getting involved in any sort of risky venture. On the whole it might be best at the moment to stick to what you know. The time for taking chances lies in the future, beyond the next few days.

17 SUNDAY   *Moon Age Day 4   Moon Sign Leo*

You are now inspired to spread your wings and some Scorpio people will be thinking seriously about changes at home. In the most extreme case a house move could be in the offing and although there is a certain amount of nostalgia to hold you back, the thought of better times to come and greater comfort could be the deciding factor.

18 MONDAY   *Moon Age Day 5   Moon Sign Leo*

At this time you might meet someone who helps you to broaden your perspectives and it looks as though you are likely to be in for a busy week. Finances are apt to be at the forefront of your thinking and there will be plenty to keep your mind occupied. Leave some time free for simple enjoyment along with your friends.

19 TUESDAY   *Moon Age Day 6   Moon Sign Virgo*

Not everything that occurs to you as being a good idea is going to be popular with those around you, especially colleagues. You will have to do a good deal of persuading if you want life to go the way you would wish. In some cases it might be better to simply follow your own course and to allow others to do the same.

20 WEDNESDAY   *Moon Age Day 7   Moon Sign Virgo*

You should do everything you can at the moment to ensure that you come across to others in a dynamic and very positive way. This can't be achieved by hiding your true feelings so you are simply going to have to show what you are made of. Once you get over your initial nerves there is very little that is presently beyond you.

21 THURSDAY   *Moon Age Day 8   Moon Sign Libra*

Certain emotions remain very close to the surface and although you might not have really thought about the situation it looks as though you are doing what you can to rebuild aspects of your romantic life. Perhaps things have been a little dull of late in that area of your life but you are certainly going to make a difference right now.

22 FRIDAY   *Moon Age Day 9   Moon Sign Libra*

What you are really looking for at the moment is personal freedom and events surrounding you today could make that possible. Drop all negative thoughts and occupy your mind with what you 'can' do. Friends should prove to be both warm and supportive just now and should be readily enlisted.

23 SATURDAY   *Moon Age Day 10   Moon Sign Scorpio*

Personal success is now very important to you and with the lunar high paying a visit you will have what it takes to keep a very high profile and to impress people with your reasoning. You should also be quite lucky under this lunar influence and you may discover that you are slightly better off than you thought.

24 SUNDAY   *Moon Age Day 11   Moon Sign Scorpio*

Your thirst for life is probably unquenchable under this influence and you should be using your creative talents to the full. This would be an excellent time to go travelling, whether or not you have arranged a journey in advance. You need fresh fields and pastures new and the power of the summer is certainly having an influence on you.

25 MONDAY   *Moon Age Day 12   Moon Sign Scorpio*

You simply refuse to be kept down this week and want to make sure that everyone is aware of your presence and your excellent ideas. Money matters should be easier to deal with and you could even discover that you are slightly better off than you expected to be. Leave boring jobs for others today and find new interests yourself.

26 TUESDAY   *Moon Age Day 13   Moon Sign Sagittarius*

Now the opportunities that stand before you are significant in proportion and there won't be a better time during June to achieve something that you have been wanting for a very long time. This demands a certain degree of courage and you should not be lacking in that department. Friends will marvel at your fortitude and determination.

27 WEDNESDAY *Moon Age Day 14   Moon Sign Sagittarius*

The Sun, now in your solar ninth house, enhances your ability to concentrate and to get on well in a professional and practical way. At the same time other planetary trends bring a real yearning for some aspects of life to be the way they were in the past. Nostalgia is fine but in the end you have to deal with the world the way it is.

28 THURSDAY   *Moon Age Day 15   Moon Sign Capricorn*

Career matters should be quite fulfilling but there isn't much doubt that the most important part of your life at the moment will be associated with romance. If you have recently started a new relationship you should be able to put on a little pressure to intensify things and Scorpio can really be the king or queen of love right now.

29 FRIDAY   *Moon Age Day 16   Moon Sign Capricorn*

Make an early start and get all unfinished jobs out of the way ahead of the weekend. It would be better if there were nothing to cloud your horizons for tomorrow, leaving you completely free to follow your own whims. From a social point of view you can paint the town red this evening so make sure you have contacted a few friends.

30 SATURDAY   *Moon Age Day 17   Moon Sign Capricorn*

Keep striving for change and variety because this will prevent you from feeling slightly lacking in vitality. It's true that you can't do everything you want in a physical or a material sense for the next couple of days but you can think and plan. By Monday you should be in a position to make ideas into realities.

July

2018

1 SUNDAY
Moon Age Day 18   Moon Sign Aquarius

Today is all about ingenuity and being in the right place to benefit from a host of new possibilities that presently surround you. Activities of all kinds are helping you to feel vital and alive, which proves to be extremely significant in the longer-term. Others are watching you closely and may be singling you out for special treatment later.

2 MONDAY
Moon Age Day 19   Moon Sign Aquarius

Professional issues are likely to be uppermost in your mind and you can make the most of some very progressive influences that come along around now. New information that comes your way needs to be thought about carefully because it is likely you can do yourself some good with a simple change of tack.

3 TUESDAY
Moon Age Day 20   Moon Sign Pisces

Cultivate the warmth and security that comes with friendship and also allow the more romantic side of your nature to show more. Partnerships are very appealing under present trends and you may discover something to your advantage from within a fond embrace. Don't get hung up on details at work and try to look at the bigger picture.

4 WEDNESDAY
Moon Age Day 21   Moon Sign Pisces

Trends at this time favour long journeys and cultural interests. If you can get away from your usual duties and responsibilities now would be a good time to do so. New experiences can be integrated into your life and the simple act of being away from your usual routine, even for a short while, might be very useful.

5 THURSDAY   *Moon Age Day 22   Moon Sign Pisces*

This is a period of expanding interests and complete concentration on specific issues. That doesn't mean you are failing to enjoy yourself too. On the contrary you will know instinctively how to compartmentalise your life in order to get the best from every situation. Take a little rest at the end of the day if you are running out of steam.

6 FRIDAY   *Moon Age Day 23   Moon Sign Aries*

You never know what you might learn and just at the moment you are fully open to all manner of new possibilities. That's why it is vitally important to keep your ears and eyes wide open and to be involved in as many conversations as possible. Even trivial gossip won't be beyond your interest at the moment.

7 SATURDAY   *Moon Age Day 24   Moon Sign Aries*

It's time for a complete change of scenery and a short break, so don't take on too much in the way of routine chores today. Keep a few hours free to accompany your partner, family members or friends on some sort of outing and try to go somewhere that stimulates your mental faculties as well as offering physical exercise.

8 SUNDAY   *Moon Age Day 25   Moon Sign Taurus*

With the lunar low comes a slightly quieter phase but one that does at least offer you the chance to look at things more deeply. Although you may be less inclined to get involved in matters for the next couple of days you are still watching. A little break will offer you the time to come up with new ideas and altered strategies.

9 MONDAY   *Moon Age Day 26   Moon Sign Taurus*

Getting your own way with others is now going to be a whole lot more difficult than it seemed to be even a couple of days ago. It might be best not to try, and to allow the water of life to flow over and around you for a few hours. If you relax and enjoy what is taking place the lunar low can prove to be a very useful and productive time.

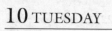

10 TUESDAY   *Moon Age Day 27   Moon Sign Gemini*

There is likely to be much of interest taking place at the present time and with everything to play for in the romantic stakes you can make the best possible impression on your partner – or someone you wish was your partner. In terms of family attachments you ought to feel very loved and quite secure now.

11 WEDNESDAY   *Moon Age Day 28   Moon Sign Gemini*

Career matters now have more going for them than might have been the case yesterday but you are still more likely to look towards your home for happiness and reassurance. It is just possible that you are feeling slightly insecure at the moment and as a Scorpio it is at such times you are most likely to seek out family members.

12 THURSDAY   *Moon Age Day 29   Moon Sign Cancer*

There are enhancements to your social life coming along any time now and you will probably also be spending a good deal of your time out of doors. The alfresco life suits you fine at this time of year and this would also be an ideal period for making changes to your domestic surroundings or, even more likely, your garden.

13 FRIDAY   *Moon Age Day 0   Moon Sign Cancer*

Travel plans should be working out well at the present time and no matter what sort of journey you are planning you should be in the market to have a good time. Try to arrange all schedules so that you can take some time out to enjoy yourself and don't allow yourself to be so busy that you fail to have a moment to spare.

14 SATURDAY   *Moon Age Day 1   Moon Sign Leo*

Around this time you may have to reassess the effect you have on other people because in some cases it might not recently have been as positive as you would have wished. When it comes to teamwork you will have to be totally honest with yourself and perhaps start to do things in a quite different way.

116

15 SUNDAY   *Moon Age Day 2   Moon Sign Leo*

Your strong opinions won't appeal to everyone today and you may need to tone down your beliefs somewhat if you are not to offer some unintended offence. In group situations you are probably not quite as adept as you were a few weeks ago but with a little effort on your part you can still win through and gain people's confidence.

16 MONDAY   *Moon Age Day 3   Moon Sign Virgo*

Now you are likely to be taking a very prominent role, especially in situations that need a dose of sound, clear thinking. People see you as capable and practical in your approach and that stands you in good stead. What a good job they can't see how little genuine confidence you have on occasion. Scorpio is the master of disguise.

17 TUESDAY   *Moon Age Day 4   Moon Sign Virgo*

Today begins a period of fairly hectic comings and goings. With little time to catch your breath you are going to have to react quickly to changing circumstances and will be at your best when people leave you in charge. What might be lacking is your usual response to family members, which is now less positive than normal.

18 WEDNESDAY   *Moon Age Day 5   Moon Sign Libra*

Group encounters and places of entertainment could be high on your agenda today, even if you are not particularly looking for either. The potential for having good times and for attracting others to you is now much better and you positively spark when in the right sort of company. This ought to make you extremely popular.

19 THURSDAY   *Moon Age Day 6   Moon Sign Libra*

Trifling matters and minor obligations might not mean all that much to you but they will keep you fairly busy today. The only frustration here is that they prevent you from doing exactly what you would wish – and this situation could continue for hours. When you finally do break free it will be obvious to everyone how relieved you are.

20 FRIDAY
Moon Age Day 7   Moon Sign Libra

Help comes from friends, and at very opportune moments. Don't assume you can do everything yourself and be willing to accept both assistance and advice when you know in your heart that you are probably out of your depth. There are unlikely to be any strings attached, even when the help comes from colleagues or associates.

21 SATURDAY
Moon Age Day 8   Moon Sign Scorpio

Your energy levels are likely to be much higher than usual and for that you can thank the lunar high. Burning the candle at both ends becomes a real possibility and having to work long and hard in order to achieve your objectives won't in the least faze you. You also know how to mix work with fun at this most interesting time.

22 SUNDAY
Moon Age Day 9   Moon Sign Scorpio

You should find more than a little good fortune coming your way at the moment and some of the benefits come from quite unexpected directions. Back your hunches and use them to your advantage, also drawing on that almost psychic quality you possess. Money could be easier to make now but it's also much easier to spend.

23 MONDAY
Moon Age Day 10   Moon Sign Sagittarius

Friends are going to be extremely important to you right now and will bring some real sunshine into your life. Speaking of sunshine, the summer is now really playing a part in your thinking, even if it is only on a subconscious level. Try to make the most of the good weather and long days by getting out into the garden or the countryside.

24 TUESDAY
Moon Age Day 11   Moon Sign Sagittarius

Look out for a new phase of major developments regarding your career, as well as new possibilities cropping up in group-based social projects. You tend to be quite practical at the best of times but will be especially so with the Sun in your solar tenth house. Be especially kind today to a friend who is more troubled than you think.

25 WEDNESDAY *Moon Age Day 12   Moon Sign Capricorn*

Casual contacts might not seem to be too important at the moment but they have a greater significance than seems to be the case. You can't afford to overlook details either because these too are going to have a bearing on your life. The more you get things right first time now, the better will be the results in a week or two.

26 THURSDAY *Moon Age Day 13   Moon Sign Capricorn*

Be on the lookout for new opportunities during this part of the week and leave no stone unturned when it comes to seeking possibilities and adventures for the future. Scorpios who have chosen this period to take a holiday are especially fortunate, but even short trips can bring handsome rewards at the moment.

27 FRIDAY *Moon Age Day 14   Moon Sign Capricorn*

Certain major accomplishments remain possible and it could seem as though some of the help you receive is divinely inspired. Being a Scorpio you are quite used to having to work hard for almost everything you get but the planets are lending a significant hand at the moment. It's now up to you to do your bit.

28 SATURDAY *Moon Age Day 15   Moon Sign Aquarius*

Don't expect it to be easy to get on with everyone today, especially those who seem to be awkward for no real reason. Nevertheless you will need to keep your cool and be as charming and polite as possible. Not everyone seems to be working for your good at the moment but you can ignore the odd misery.

29 SUNDAY *Moon Age Day 16   Moon Sign Aquarius*

You could discover today that less self-determination is required, simply because you are more or less forced to follow the orders of others. This is not a problem when you agree with them but can certainly cause you some aggravation when you know that you could do much better if you were left to your own devices.

30 MONDAY

Moon Age Day 17   Moon Sign Pisces

What is needed, especially in discussions, is a much lighter touch and a warmth and regard for others. Take time out to make sure that someone important is aware of your concern because you can't take their attitude for granted. It isn't so much a case of doing any more but rather making it plain how you feel.

31 TUESDAY

Moon Age Day 18   Moon Sign Pisces

Pressures should ease in your professional life and if you are between jobs at the moment you should look more carefully than usual at any opportunities that come your way. Self-employed Scorpios may be the luckiest of all because this is a time when you are able to gain new and more lucrative strings to your bow.

August 2018

1 WEDNESDAY ☿ *Moon Age Day 19 Moon Sign Pisces*

Project yourself as much as possible today and take on new responsibilities if they interest you in any way. You are probably not working to your full potential at the present time and there is more that you can do to promote your own interests. Unusual or surprising responses work best when you are dealing with original sorts of people.

2 THURSDAY ☿ *Moon Age Day 20 Moon Sign Aries*

This is a time when you will be setting out to improve your mind as much as possible. The more you stretch yourself, the greater are likely to be the ultimate rewards. Any sort of puzzle will probably have a particular fascination for you under present trends and you seem to be especially motivated by solving some of life's mysteries.

3 FRIDAY ☿ *Moon Age Day 21 Moon Sign Aries*

You could be slightly sensitive to criticism right now, and this might explain why you will withdraw from certain issues if you suspect that not everyone is on your side. These are likely to be more personal that professional situations and it could be that you are reacting too harshly to nothing tangible. It is important to be optimistic.

4 SATURDAY ☿ *Moon Age Day 22 Moon Sign Taurus*

This is a time to pace yourself and to avoid taking on so much that you become fatigued by it all. One thing at a time seems to be the best adage for you and you would be well advised to leave really arduous tasks until a later date. What others are up to right now is probably not your concern so curb your curiosity.

5 SUNDAY ☿ *Moon Age Day 23 Moon Sign Taurus*

Some plans might have to be totally abandoned or at the very least postponed until a more sensible time. Allow your friends to do things for you and accept that relationships are a two-way street and that people often want to help you out. This is not a day to be too proud or to turn down the chance to be spoiled in some way.

6 MONDAY ☿ *Moon Age Day 24 Moon Sign Gemini*

Don't allow your present need for peace and harmony to stifle your creative instincts or to prevent you from speaking out if you feel strongly about a particular issue. It would also be quite easy today to allow others to take advantage of your good nature so guard against this in almost every situation.

7 TUESDAY ☿ *Moon Age Day 25 Moon Sign Gemini*

If you are at work today you can make great gains because most of the positive trends at the moment are more likely to affect your professional life than your personal one. All the same you can enjoy yourself and have fun, especially with good friends, even if there are a few issues to deal with as far as family relationships are concerned.

8 WEDNESDAY ☿ *Moon Age Day 26 Moon Sign Gemini*

Emotions can now be very close to the surface, especially when you are at home. And it isn't just that you are likely to fire off without thinking. This could lead to unnecessary misunderstandings and even arguments. Scorpio doesn't argue all that often but when you do get in gear you can sometimes be quite vitriolic.

9 THURSDAY ☿ *Moon Age Day 27 Moon Sign Cancer*

You may have a talent for drawing friends together, which also means being able to get them to follow your lead. Get on side with those who seem to have a good understanding of what is needed, especially at work, and do what you can to ease the problems of a friend who is going through a difficult time.

10 FRIDAY   ☿   *Moon Age Day 28   Moon Sign Cancer*

Be sure that you are not being led up the garden path by false promises. There are some really duplicitous people around now who must be avoided at all costs. Your intuition is your best guide at present and it is unlikely to let you down. In romantic terms you are now more powerful and dominant than you think.

11 SATURDAY   ☿   *Moon Age Day 0   Moon Sign Leo*

Your professional life should be undergoing a degree of good fortune, though you are less likely to register this at the weekend. If you do work today you should take someone higher up the tree than you are into your confidence and in any situation you should not be afraid to speak out when you know a plan of action is brilliant.

12 SUNDAY   ☿   *Moon Age Day 1   Moon Sign Leo*

This is likely to be one of the better days of the month as far as social pleasures are concerned. Your mind has been turning this way and that – trying to make sense of all that is taking place around you but now you are likely to be more settled and content with your lot. Spending time with family members could appeal today.

13 MONDAY   ☿   *Moon Age Day 2   Moon Sign Virgo*

An underlying theme of renewal now prevails. There are certain issues in your life that need reappraising and that is what you tend to focus on at the moment. This stage of the month also means a better financial understanding on your part and a renewal of a promise that has great personal implications.

14 TUESDAY   ☿   *Moon Age Day 3   Moon Sign Virgo*

More personal freedom becomes possible and you seem to be quite determined to have your own way – especially where the organisation of your life is concerned. You can be nobody's pawn under present trends and if you feel you are being put upon in any way you will dig in your heels. New characters are about to enter your life.

15 WEDNESDAY ☿ *Moon Age Day 4   Moon Sign Libra*

Right now you are a socially motivated person and would be best suited to working in groups. The thought of going it alone, though appealing, isn't going to get you the accolades that come when you are involved with others. Some patience is necessary because you don't suffer fools gladly and there are one or two around.

16 THURSDAY ☿ *Moon Age Day 5   Moon Sign Libra*

This would be a great time to extend yourself in social situations and to make others sit up and take notice of your all-round personality. When it comes to solving problems you are likely to be second-to-none and you won't have any difficulty breaking new ground or acquiring skills you didn't have before.

17 FRIDAY ☿ *Moon Age Day 6   Moon Sign Scorpio*

What really matters today is the way you can get others on your side, which will prove to be of great importance if you want to try something new and revolutionary. Achieving any sort of goal ought to be easier with the lunar high around and even people who can often behave in an awkward manner will be more helpful.

18 SATURDAY ☿ *Moon Age Day 7   Moon Sign Scorpio*

You could feel restless and impatient to do something quite different. Most of your planetary positions at the moment will cry out for you to make changes, which are also good because they take your mind off issues that are not half as difficult as you seem to painting them at the moment. The busier you are, the happier you will be.

19 SUNDAY *Moon Age Day 8   Moon Sign Sagittarius*

You have a strong focus on particular objectives and can concentrate on these, almost to the exclusion of everything else. That's fine as far as it goes but it does mean that on some occasions you could fail to see the wood for the trees. What is really needed is a more across-the-board attitude and great flexibility for most of the day.

20 MONDAY   *Moon Age Day 9   Moon Sign Sagittarius*

You should particularly enjoy being out there in good company this week and the show starts today. There are gains to be made by pushing yourself forward and by being willing to act as spokesperson for groups or organisations. People will probably rely heavily on you today but you have what it takes to come through smiling.

21 TUESDAY   *Moon Age Day 10   Moon Sign Sagittarius*

Things should continue to be quite eventful and it looks as though you will be encountering a little more in the way of general good luck than might sometimes be the case. You can afford to back your hunches most of the time at present but you also need to employ a good deal of common sense regarding relationship issues.

22 WEDNESDAY   *Moon Age Day 11   Moon Sign Capricorn*

Your instincts are well honed today and you could do worse than to follow them under most circumstances. Look out for people who might be of use to you professionally, but take care about signing documents or taking on commitments without first looking very carefully. Someone might be getting on your nerves.

23 THURSDAY   *Moon Age Day 12   Moon Sign Capricorn*

Don't allow others to misunderstand you. It will probably be necessary to explain yourself more than once and under all circumstances you must make sure that those around you are in no doubt about your point of view. In matters of the heart you show yourself to be a true romantic and should pick up accolades as a result.

24 FRIDAY   *Moon Age Day 13   Moon Sign Aquarius*

A matter at work could be going slightly off course and although there is nothing seriously wrong, this is the time to get the train back on to the track. Distractions come thick and fast, some of which seem certain to throw you into a state of disarray but the truth is that you have focus and staying power. It's simply a case of employing it.

25 SATURDAY   *Moon Age Day 14   Moon Sign Aquarius*

The past seems to have a great deal to do with your present thoughts, perhaps because you are dwelling on issues from years ago that seem to have a bearing on the present. In reality you would be better off judging everything on its present merits and leaving nostalgia of any sort alone. Your attitude should be realistic and totally up-to-date.

26 SUNDAY   *Moon Age Day 15   Moon Sign Aquarius*

In order to feel at your best today you require evidence of security. You need to know that others are rooting for you and that personal attachments are as sound as they can be. Once you have satisfied yourself you should be in a much better position to push forward positively and to enjoy fully what this August Sunday has to offer.

27 MONDAY   *Moon Age Day 16   Moon Sign Pisces*

This may not be the most enjoyable part of the month for relationships, mainly because you don't seem to be able to knock people off their feet as well as you did a couple of weeks ago. This almost certainly has little to do with your own capabilities and is related to situations that are totally beyond your control.

28 TUESDAY   *Moon Age Day 17   Moon Sign Pisces*

Don't be shy about your feelings today and although it might not always be easy to do so you need to keep talking and to explain yourself fully. In some ways you become slightly more impulsive and will have less of a tendency to dig yourself into your own little hole. The Scorpion begins to emerge from its nest.

29 WEDNESDAY   *Moon Age Day 18   Moon Sign Aries*

Right now you have a strong need for reassurance, though only up to a point. As the day advances so you should be getting more and more confident and will gradually rely less on the good offices of others. Any form of travel is likely to appeal to you at the moment and a late summer holiday would be ideal for most Scorpios.

30 THURSDAY   *Moon Age Day 19   Moon Sign Aries*

At home you are now a good diplomat and should be in a position to sort out some sort of disagreement or situation that has caused a rift. You will also be open and honest at work but it is important to remember that you must avoid taking sides in disputes. Instead, stand aside and arbitrate.

31 FRIDAY   *Moon Age Day 20   Moon Sign Aries*

Any attempt to dominate relationships will be more or less doomed to failure at present. The more humble you appear, the greater is the chance that you will bring others round to your point of view. There is something very impulsive about Scorpio at the present time, which is fine just as long as you realise this and keep control.

September 2018

1 SATURDAY
Moon Age Day 21   Moon Sign Taurus

This could turn out to be quite a dull day but it really depends on the amount of effort you are willing to put in. Don't go to too much trouble because with the lunar low around even if you move mountains you might find nothing of much interest under them. Simply accept what life offers you and keep your eyes open for later.

2 SUNDAY
Moon Age Day 22   Moon Sign Taurus

There could be challenges to your confidence arising around this time. Not everyone appears to have too much faith in your abilities but much of the problem exists in your mind rather than in reality. Let others do some of the hard work today. The responsibility will do them good and the break from hard work will benefit you.

3 MONDAY
Moon Age Day 23   Moon Sign Gemini

Friendships are positively highlighted today and you can bring a touch of magic and warmth to both old and new encounters. People will be pleased to have you close to them and should be willing to divulge their most intimate secrets. You should find yourself in a positive and generally optimistic frame of mind.

4 TUESDAY
Moon Age Day 24   Moon Sign Gemini

Your influence on life is quite noteworthy today. There are gains to be made on the financial front but the most important steps you take have little or nothing to do with money. Love is a strong factor in your thinking and decision-making and you should have what it takes to increase your personal popularity across the board.

5 WEDNESDAY   *Moon Age Day 25   Moon Sign Cancer*

You can do well in finances at this stage of the week. Perhaps money comes from unexpected directions or you may be paid back fully in terms of a loan you made. This would be a good day to sign contracts or to take on new financial deals because you have it about you to read the small print very carefully.

6 THURSDAY   *Moon Age Day 26   Moon Sign Cancer*

A preoccupation with the past may dominate your day and when Scorpio starts looking back it can have a great bearing on the present. Don't necessarily assume that because something turned out in a particular way before it will do so again now. Try to keep your mind focused on what is around the next corner and welcome it.

7 FRIDAY   *Moon Age Day 27   Moon Sign Leo*

You can look forward to a generally warm response when it comes to social encounters and matters associated with romance. There could be attention coming your way from a more or less unexpected direction and it looks as though you will be quite settled in your affections. You may even learn to like someone you once hated.

8 SATURDAY   *Moon Age Day 28   Moon Sign Leo*

Relationships get a further boost under present planetary trends. This may turn out to be one of the most romantic interludes of the year and you will certainly be on the receiving end of some great compliments. You could be slightly bad tempered when you are faced with people who seem determined to do stupid things.

9 SUNDAY   *Moon Age Day 0   Moon Sign Virgo*

Your love life should be eventful and enjoyable around now. Scorpios who are involved in deep attachments should find the heat rising and if you are looking for a new attachment you should keep your eyes open today. Sometimes romance can spring up from the most surprising and least likely directions.

10 MONDAY   *Moon Age Day 1   Moon Sign Virgo*

You may find you are unable to cope if you take on too many responsibilities at this time. This is not to suggest that you are failing to do what is necessary to keep forward motion going in your life. It's really just a case of choosing your activities carefully and leaving some of the major tasks until another more positive day.

11 TUESDAY   *Moon Age Day 2   Moon Sign Libra*

Try to broaden your horizons as much as possible now and make the most of any remaining good weather in order to get out of the house. Do things that you find stimulating and interesting, rather than sticking to mundane domestic chores that will frustrate you.

12 WEDNESDAY   *Moon Age Day 3   Moon Sign Libra*

You are better off today when you find yourself amongst groups of people or in situations where sharing becomes a possibility. Going it alone is not to be recommended for the moment and you will be doing all you can to support and encourage people who may not have been having a good time recently.

13 THURSDAY   *Moon Age Day 4   Moon Sign Scorpio*

You now have exactly what it takes to get the sort of results you are looking for. There is everything to play for while the lunar high is around and since it continues into Friday you can use at least part of today in order to get yourself ready for a flurry of activity that will surround your career tomorrow.

14 FRIDAY   *Moon Age Day 5   Moon Sign Scorpio*

Your spirits are lifted no end and you positively fly towards your objectives on a day that offers so much in terms of energy and enthusiasm. People who matter the most are definitely going to be on your side at the present time and those who are not won't be significant. Play your natural good luck for all it is worth at this time.

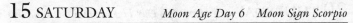

15 SATURDAY   *Moon Age Day 6   Moon Sign Scorpio*

Discussions with others may bring a few disappointments. This is not a strong trend and it doesn't last long but for today at least you could discover that you are being misunderstood or, worse still, not listened to at all. Try to sort out the issues if you get the opportunity to.

16 SUNDAY   *Moon Age Day 7   Moon Sign Sagittarius*

Scorpio now becomes much more innovative and you will be looking repeatedly at new ways of getting on well, especially in a financial sense. Some things still come hard to you but you overcome obstacles fairly easily and show the world at large that you are equal to just about any task you choose to take on.

17 MONDAY   *Moon Age Day 8   Moon Sign Sagittarius*

Just like that feisty little insect for which your zodiac sign is named, you are inclined to hide in dark corners and to come out fighting at the first indication that someone is threatening you. This sort of behaviour is fine under some circumstances but is certainly not necessary at the moment. An open attitude is called for.

18 TUESDAY   *Moon Age Day 9   Moon Sign Capricorn*

Being naturally courageous you are more willing than your friends to do something that is just slightly dangerous. That's fine just as long as the risks you take are calculated. What you don't need today is to put yourself in peril for no good reason. In all probability the person you most want to impress at the moment is yourself.

19 WEDNESDAY   *Moon Age Day 10   Moon Sign Capricorn*

The domestic scene is one of your best areas at the moment but it is far from being the only one. Friends make demands on your time and your experience. It looks as though you will have little time to call your own but since you are likely to be quite happy with your lot you should show a contented and happy face to the world.

20 THURSDAY   *Moon Age Day 11   Moon Sign Aquarius*

Although you are pushing ahead with various plans at the moment some of these are likely to be going slightly wrong. You will need to keep your wits about you and it will be necessary to react quickly in order to keep things in line. Part of the problem could arise from constantly having to repeat the same job.

21 FRIDAY   *Moon Age Day 12   Moon Sign Aquarius*

As is often the case you can be highly secretive at the moment and will need to share your ideas and opinions more if you want to get others onside. This isn't especially easy for you and is made all the more difficult if you suspect that someone is trying to rob you of your originality. What you need most is to curb your natural scepticism.

22 SATURDAY   *Moon Age Day 13   Moon Sign Aquarius*

You might feel a compulsion to spend time on your own, mainly because you need space to think and can't do so when there are people constantly chatting in your ear. These periods of withdrawal are nothing unusual for Scorpio and are part of the way you keep your head straight. Money matters look settled.

23 SUNDAY   *Moon Age Day 14   Moon Sign Pisces*

In all probability you long to change things significantly – by travel if necessary. This is possible but rather less than likely, mainly because you feel there is too much to do. Perhaps you are overstressing your own importance in certain situations. It's time to delegate and to allow others to take on some more of the responsibility.

24 MONDAY   *Moon Age Day 15   Moon Sign Pisces*

You clearly want to get ahead at the start of this week, especially in a practical sense, but there are situations that need constant checking and verification. This slows you down and can make certain aspects of life a little tedious. What you need is something different to do once the demands of work are out of the way.

25 TUESDAY   *Moon Age Day 16   Moon Sign Aries*

Success in your career now comes through a combination of originality and your present ability to think deeply about almost everything. Although you are better at co-operating today it is quite likely that you will still actively choose to do most things yourself and will avoid getting involved in the schemes and machinations of others.

26 WEDNESDAY   *Moon Age Day 17   Moon Sign Aries*

The accent now is on close, personal relationships much more than on casual attachments. You won't be keen to try out new situations and possibilities, at least not until you are very sure that the basis of your life is solid. Scorpio is not at its must humorous at the moment but you will have your moments.

27 THURSDAY   *Moon Age Day 18   Moon Sign Aries*

Getting out and about does increase your chances of learning things that are going to be of significance to you in a general sense and it also broadens your horizons at a time when you are quite insular. The only difficulty is forcing yourself to do things that you instinctively feel will be hard and a waste of effort.

28 FRIDAY   *Moon Age Day 19   Moon Sign Taurus*

The lunar low says that you must be patient and allow things to mature in their own good time. What you can't afford to do today or tomorrow is to push issues too hard. For one thing you would soon run out of energy and could find things crowding in on you when you least expect it. At least finances should look fairly settled.

29 SATURDAY   *Moon Age Day 20   Moon Sign Taurus*

Your personal influence regarding everyday issues is somewhat diminished and this alone could lead to further frustrations. The way round the problem is to maintain your sense of humour and to show just how resilient you can be. There are always alternatives and a little adversity allows you to find them.

30 SUNDAY   *Moon Age Day 21   Moon Sign Gemini*

It may not seem that you are really at your best in social situations but others find you fun to be around and your present sardonic sense of humour will be particularly attractive. The results are that you have a good time, almost despite yourself, and that you continue to impress people even when there is no real reason to do so.

October 2018

1 MONDAY
Moon Age Day 22   Moon Sign Gemini

You remain dynamic and enthusiastic. Not only do you have all the vitality and power you could require, you also have masses of charm and a winning personality that nobody could ignore. This really is a major-league time for you and should be treated as one of the best phases of the year in an all-round sense.

2 TUESDAY
Moon Age Day 23   Moon Sign Cancer

Your partner could be quite difficult to please for the next couple of days and what might make matters worse is that the Sun is still in your solar twelfth house. This means you are slightly lacking in tact and won't have quite the level of confidence in your own abilities and opinions that is often the case.

3 WEDNESDAY
Moon Age Day 24   Moon Sign Cancer

Partnerships are now favourably highlighted and co-operation becomes the unequivocal key to success. Out here in the middle of the week you should be quite satisfied with your efforts and you seem to have what it takes to be especially popular when you are in good company. Get on with jobs you find interesting and stimulating.

4 THURSDAY
Moon Age Day 25   Moon Sign Leo

Get down to brass tacks today as far as money is concerned and order your finances in a very positive sort of way. This is also a time during which you can afford to indulge yourself more than you normally would and you should also find that your friends are anxious to show you their generosity.

5 FRIDAY
Moon Age Day 26   Moon Sign Leo

You work best when you are involved in an interesting social environment and as a result you might not be trying too hard to get much done in a practical sense today. Your judgement is sound and you are able to get onside with the sort of people who rarely fail to get things done. You may even decide to follow their lead later.

6 SATURDAY
Moon Age Day 27   Moon Sign Virgo

You are probably your own worst critic today, which is something of a shame at a time when things ought to be going very well for you. If you do lack patience with yourself you will not do as well as you would if you remained optimistic regarding the outcome of any situation. Keep abreast of local news and views at this time.

7 SUNDAY
Moon Age Day 28   Moon Sign Virgo

Romantically and personally you are likely to be on a winning streak and the intensity of positive situations is now likely to be so great you would be quite unlikely to miss out on any of the benefits coming in your direction. Stand up for friends in disputes but wherever possible talk your way out of awkward situations.

8 MONDAY
Moon Age Day 29   Moon Sign Virgo

Home and family are vital issues for you at the best of times but they seem to be more important than ever as the Moon moves on in your chart later today. You will most likely be entering a new phase in terms of a personal attachment and younger family members will now be more likely to turn to you for practical help and advice.

9 TUESDAY
Moon Age Day 0   Moon Sign Libra

Today you are more inclined to see things in terms of the way they will have a bearing on your personal and family life. The world beyond your own door is not quite as important as might sometimes be the case and you become a slightly more private sort of person. This is not at all unusual for Scorpio from time to time.

10 WEDNESDAY   *Moon Age Day 1   Moon Sign Libra*

The focus is on finance and it looks as though you will already be finding ways to improve things, even if the plans you put into action today won't mature for a week or two. At the same time you now tend to be slightly more outgoing and there are likely to be invitations around that will draw you out of your own little corner.

11 THURSDAY   *Moon Age Day 2   Moon Sign Scorpio*

Today you are calling the shots and the lunar high brings the best possible potential for a time of fun and happy encounters. Don't be too keen to keep busy all the time because you are very socially inclined at present and will want to please yourself. Break out while you can and get well away from the usual concerns of a routine Thursday.

12 FRIDAY   *Moon Age Day 3   Moon Sign Scorpio*

You should be feeling very energetic and you won't be at all tardy when it comes to getting involved in anything that stretches your abilities and offers excitement. Your financial standing should be slightly improved – or else you begin to discover that you can raise money in previously unknown ways.

13 SATURDAY   *Moon Age Day 4   Moon Sign Sagittarius*

Don't rely entirely on your intuition when it comes to important matters. As a rule your almost psychic nature is your best guide but this probably isn't the case now. It is facts and figures that really count, together with the tried-and-tested advice of people who have done the same thing you are facing now time and again.

14 SUNDAY   *Moon Age Day 5   Moon Sign Sagittarius*

A significant boost to teamwork and group activities comes along today, courtesy of the rapidly moving Moon. In any situation it is important not to let your own perceived limitations hold you back but rather to have confidence in your ability to learn as you go along. Experience is a fine thing but it has to come from doing a job.

15 MONDAY   *Moon Age Day 6   Moon Sign Capricorn*

There could be some pressure upon you now to rethink your strategies regarding work-based issues but it might be best to stick to your own guns with things as they are in a planetary sense. Of course you need to show yourself willing to listen to another point of view but in the end it is your opinions that really count.

16 TUESDAY   *Moon Age Day 7   Moon Sign Capricorn*

There could be a few practical mishaps today and you might be too inclined to rush things. Try to settle to what you are doing and make sure you do things one at a time. There ought to be a great deal of attention coming to you from people who are especially fond of you and practical help is in place if you need it.

17 WEDNESDAY   *Moon Age Day 8   Moon Sign Capricorn*

When it comes to your social life you will be enjoying a happy and eventful period around now. Any sort of dialogue between yourself and others can provide you with new ideas and a renewed sense of purpose regarding practical issues. You will also be doing what you can to create comfortable surroundings at home.

18 THURSDAY   *Moon Age Day 9   Moon Sign Aquarius*

You might be forced to change your mind about something major today. There are some unusual situations coming to light and all sorts of odd coincidences could crowd in on your day. Don't let them spook you and merely treat them as signposts towards a better future – if you take note of them.

19 FRIDAY   *Moon Age Day 10   Moon Sign Aquarius*

As the days go on you will discover that your ego is growing stronger and that you develop better and better ways to make people take notice of you. This process begins now as several planets edge themselves onward in your solar chart. People might not be hanging on your every word but they are at least looking your way.

20 SATURDAY   *Moon Age Day 11   Moon Sign Pisces*

Keep well organised and it looks as though you won't go far wrong. Although there is no particular rush about life just at the moment you will recognise that it would be best to grab opportunities whilst they are around. Friends will be equally busy and might not always be able to drop everything just to suit your particular needs.

21 SUNDAY   *Moon Age Day 12   Moon Sign Pisces*

It's time to be broadening your personal horizons. It's a fact about autumn-born Scorpio that when many people are starting to slow down for the winter, you are just getting into gear. The thought of shorter days and colder weather does little or nothing to dent your enthusiasm and you should be especially optimistic today.

22 MONDAY   *Moon Age Day 13   Moon Sign Pisces*

Keep your eyes open because there are new opportunities about, all of which seem custom-made to bring more fun into your life. You are now much more resilient and are determined to break down barriers if necessary in order to get where you want to be. Romance is especially well starred at present.

23 TUESDAY   *Moon Age Day 14   Moon Sign Aries*

What you really manage to do at the moment is to get the very best out of almost everyone you come across. Part of this is down to astrological influences but it can be aided by your own attitude, which is now positive and determined. Get in touch with someone who lives at a distance and arrange to visit them.

24 WEDNESDAY   *Moon Age Day 15   Moon Sign Aries*

Get out there and make new friends. It is very important at the moment to make the best of impression on just about anyone and this is going to be especially important at work. Mixing business with pleasure isn't something you do all as a rule but it can stand you in good stead under present planetary trends.

25 THURSDAY   *Moon Age Day 16   Moon Sign Taurus*

This brief period of inactivity is simply a slight pause on the otherwise presently smooth road that is your life. Let the traffic flow on for a while as you stand and watch contentedly. Frustration will only follow if you insist on try to do too much at a time when the prevailing planetary influences are telling you to preserve your energy.

26 FRIDAY   *Moon Age Day 17   Moon Sign Taurus*

Although it might not seem to be the case as the day gets started most of your efforts around now have success written all over them. A break from everyday routines is still recommended but not so that you can continue to watch and wait. On the contrary you now need to be doing different and stimulating things, alongside your friends.

27 SATURDAY   *Moon Age Day 18   Moon Sign Gemini*

The Sun is now in your solar first house and brings with it that part of the year during which you can be expected to make significant gains and to be at your best in most situations. You ought to be feeling far more confident than you were a couple of weeks ago and part of this has to do with your ability to work through sticky patches.

28 SUNDAY   *Moon Age Day 19   Moon Sign Gemini*

You might sense that in some ways a more frugal approach is necessary and if so you will be reining in your spending. It is possible that this attitude has something to do with dawning realisation that Christmas is not far away, or it may simply be that you have a project in mind that will require money.

29 MONDAY   *Moon Age Day 20   Moon Sign Cancer*

You look and feel strong, which is why almost everyone takes it for granted that you could achieve almost anything. There is no point in telling them that this is not the case, so you may as well believe it yourself. Don't get tied down today with pointless routines but take gains where you find them and push for what you really want.

30 TUESDAY   *Moon Age Day 21   Moon Sign Cancer*

Give and take is important at home, especially if certain family members are behaving in a less that typical way. Fortunately this is not likely to be the case in a romantic sense. In this area of your life you know exactly what to say and will also have a good idea about what makes your partner tick. A timely gift can make all the difference.

31 WEDNESDAY   *Moon Age Day 22   Moon Sign Cancer*

Remove yourself from confrontational situations because you really don't need any arguments in your life just now. You want to be friends with everyone, something that might prove to be difficult but certainly not impossible. They say it takes two to tango and if you don't want to fall out with anyone, nothing will persuade you to do so.

November 2018

1 THURSDAY
Moon Age Day 23   Moon Sign Leo

You can now expect to be taking a hands-on role when it comes to creating your own future. Scorpio sometimes feels itself locked up in the needs and opinions of other people but this is far less likely to be the case during the first half of November. A new month means new perspectives, and the necessary energy to get things moving.

2 FRIDAY
Moon Age Day 24   Moon Sign Leo

More than ever today you seem to be taken up with practical ideas and with getting things done as efficiently as you can. You might have to put one or two personal plans on hold because you can't do everything at the same time, no matter how much you try. Pace yourself and try to get as much fun as possible from the day.

3 SATURDAY
Moon Age Day 25   Moon Sign Virgo

You should find that you now have greater control over your life and its circumstances. This is part of the legacy of the first house Sun you are enjoying at the moment and you probably find yourself in the midst of an eventful and generally exciting period. Whilst others are gearing down for winter you are as lively as a cricket.

4 SUNDAY
Moon Age Day 26   Moon Sign Virgo

Your powers are generally good and you keep your wits about you under most circumstances now. You can be of tremendous help to your friends and even to people you barely know at all. That's because your powers of discrimination are good and you are quite happy to pass on your acquired wisdom to others.

5 MONDAY
Moon Age Day 27   Moon Sign Libra

The influence you have over certain people is now less certain than it appeared to be a day or two ago. Before you start anything new, especially if it means relying on others, do make sure that the co-operation you need is going to be forthcoming. Slight embarrassment could be the result of taking people for granted today.

6 TUESDAY
Moon Age Day 28   Moon Sign Libra

It would be best not to expect too much from others at this time. When it comes to getting things done you might decide to go it alone and some relationships could be fraught with complications. In the main, life is still going your way and despite minor frustrations you will win through in most important situations.

7 WEDNESDAY
Moon Age Day 0   Moon Sign Scorpio

Now you can break through barriers that may have stood before you for months or even years. Having done so you move into new pastures altogether and can achieve some of the successes that might have eluded you for a while. Seek out someone you haven't seen for ages and renew your contact with them.

8 THURSDAY
Moon Age Day 1   Moon Sign Scorpio

Communication remains the important component of your life, not just because of the lunar high but also on account of the position of the Sun. If you remain quiet today nobody will know what you want and since they find you so charming at the moment getting their assistance to further your own plans is simply a matter of asking.

9 FRIDAY
Moon Age Day 2   Moon Sign Sagittarius

You have a good mind for business and the decisions you make at this time tend to be shot through with perception and wisdom. Avoid confrontations at work by finding ways to agree with others while at the same time managing to get your own way. A little psychology can go a long way right now and this is something you are good at.

143

10 SATURDAY　　*Moon Age Day 3　　Moon Sign Sagittarius*

It you are at work you can expect steady and smooth progress, matched by a fairly uneventful but generally peaceful time at home. This may not be the most exciting period of the year but it is solid and dependable. If there is one thing Scorpio respects it is the ability to know what is coming and you also like others to be as reliable as you are.

11 SUNDAY　　*Moon Age Day 4　　Moon Sign Sagittarius*

The focus is now much more likely to be on your public persona. You won't be hiding your natural abilities but neither will you be brash or outspoken. The combination of charisma, charm and practical common sense that you display now and during the coming week should assure you of great popularity.

12 MONDAY　　*Moon Age Day 5　　Moon Sign Capricorn*

In the middle of a phase of enhanced social activity there ought to be plenty of opportunities for light relief and for a relaxation where more serious matters are concerned. In many situations you should be able to find the answers you need quickly and are unlikely to be spending endless hours mulling things over.

13 TUESDAY　　*Moon Age Day 6　　Moon Sign Capricorn*

This may be the best time of all to confide your feelings to loved ones and to get on with sorting things out as far as your home is concerned. Be as sympathetic as you can to those who are presently having difficulties and show just how helpful the sign of Scorpio can be. Avoid pointless routines today because they would bore you.

14 WEDNESDAY　　*Moon Age Day 7　　Moon Sign Aquarius*

Practical affairs should be looking up. Now is a good time for consolidation as you find the time you need to let others know the way your mind is working on many different levels. Simply sitting around and talking can be very important and you can catch up on all sorts of news you didn't know before.

15 THURSDAY
Moon Age Day 8   Moon Sign Aquarius

Look out for a few harsh words today, possibly between yourself and your life partner. If this does happen, find out what is causing the irritation and that means taking time out from a busy schedule to ask a few questions. Any misunderstandings can then be dealt with in no time at all.

16 FRIDAY
Moon Age Day 9   Moon Sign Aquarius

Don't get too carried away today because although life looks exciting you also need to focus on what is really important. There are too many distractions around at present and these could cause you to miss something that could bring in money and opportunities later. All that's needed is for you to keep your eyes and ears open.

17 SATURDAY
☿   *Moon Age Day 10   Moon Sign Pisces*

It is clear that you still want to have fun and that you will also be keen to involve as many people as you can in some of your ingenious schemes. Not all of these are going to work out quite the way you might have intended but even if you only succeed in ten percent you will end November somewhat better off than you began it.

18 SUNDAY
☿   *Moon Age Day 11   Moon Sign Pisces*

You really need to feel useful today and will be doing all you can to be supportive of both colleagues and friends. Once the routine aspects of the day are dealt with the time will be right to have some fun. Involve family members if you can but it's especially important to include your partner.

19 MONDAY
☿   *Moon Age Day 12   Moon Sign Aries*

The time seems right to tighten up certain securities – which ought to make you feel more comfortable with your life generally. Not everyone will have your best interests at heart right now but you are shrewd and attentive, which means the chances of anyone duping you are as near to zero as makes no odds.

20 TUESDAY ☿ *Moon Age Day 13   Moon Sign Aries*

There isn't much doubt about your ability to get on extremely well with those people you care about the most but what might be even more important is your response to virtual strangers. The usual Scorpio suspicion seems to be taking a holiday and you make new friends at every turn. One or two of these could prove to be significant.

21 WEDNESDAY ☿ *Moon Age Day 14   Moon Sign Taurus*

The lunar low is underpinned this month by topsy-turvy influences, some of which come like a bolt from the blue and knock your reasoning sideways. Try a few alternative points of view and examine situations carefully before you take any sort of prohibitive action. If it were possible to stand still altogether you should do it.

22 THURSDAY ☿ *Moon Age Day 15   Moon Sign Taurus*

The go-getting side of your personality remains strong, even if you find it somewhat difficult to go and get precisely what you want for today at least. By tomorrow everything should be more or less back to normal, except for the fact that the Sun is moving out of your solar first house and into the somewhat more solid second.

23 FRIDAY ☿ *Moon Age Day 16   Moon Sign Taurus*

Today you should be striving for a peaceful and contented home-life. While this is yours for the taking it is unlikely to be the end of the story because as soon as you sit down in your favourite chair you will become restless and will want to be on the move again. Relatives will marvel at your restlessness.

24 SATURDAY ☿ *Moon Age Day 17   Moon Sign Gemini*

You have what it takes to show yourself in a new light, particularly to people who haven't noticed you at all so far this year. Your energy levels are likely to be high and you revel in any opportunity to get involved with social events. Although you will be extremely busy you still seem to find sufficient time to do almost every you wish.

25 SUNDAY   ☿ *Moon Age Day 18   Moon Sign Gemini*

If you want to make sure that everything you say is clearly understood you might have to make your position extremely clear. Don't worry that others will tire of hearing your voice. On the contrary you are going to be just about as popular as it is possible to be, whilst at the same time getting most of what you want from life.

26 MONDAY   ☿ *Moon Age Day 19   Moon Sign Cancer*

If business or practical issues are up for discussion you are likely to be taking a leading role. You seem to have some really good ideas at the moment and will be quite happy to throw these in for what they are worth. Don't expect to make too much progress in matters of love today – through no fault of your own.

27 TUESDAY   ☿ *Moon Age Day 20   Moon Sign Cancer*

With plenty of enjoyment in mind you are now slightly less likely to be thinking about progress of any sort. The one exception is possibly a desire to do well in sporting activities. Scorpio hates to be beaten and this facet of your nature is probably stronger now than would normally be the case.

28 WEDNESDAY ☿   *Moon Age Day 21   Moon Sign Leo*

What you hear from others today can contribute to the very progressive phase you are presently enjoying. The only slight fly in the ointment comes from colleagues or friends who promise more than they deliver. Keep on top of situations and when you see you can't rely on others, get cracking yourself. Your energy levels remain high.

29 THURSDAY   ☿   *Moon Age Day 22   Moon Sign Leo*

You simply want to achieve too much and as a result you might find certain projects grinding to a halt. Drop half of your expectations for the moment and concentrate on issues that are very nearly sorted. That way you will also have time to have fun, which is probably more important than anything at the end of November.

30 FRIDAY ☿ *Moon Age Day 23   Moon Sign Virgo*

Almost everything is working well for you as this most fortunate month draws to a close. The realisation that December is about to start could come as something of a shock, if only because you have been too busy to look at the calendar. Spend some time today listening carefully to the opinions of the people with whom you live.

December

2018

1 SATURDAY ☿ Moon Age Day 24 Moon Sign Virgo

This would be an ideal time to look again at your money and to decide how best you can use your resources more wisely. Be inventive when it comes to buying your Christmas gifts and don't squander cash on non-essentials. Under the present position of the Sun you should be filled with useful and quite innovative ideas.

2 SUNDAY ☿ Moon Age Day 25 Moon Sign Libra

Everything seems to focus on your love life now, and a little extra effort could prove to be quite useful. Make sure the most important person in your life knows how significant they are to you – which means telling them, of course. This is not a good period for taking those you care about for granted.

3 MONDAY ☿ Moon Age Day 26 Moon Sign Libra

Property and financial interests are now positively highlighted in your solar chart. You remain basically innovative and filled with good ideas as to how you can increase your fortune and your influence in the days ahead. If you splash out on anything around now it could well be a gift for your partner.

4 TUESDAY ☿ Moon Age Day 27 Moon Sign Scorpio

You should be at the very forefront of anything that is happening around you – mostly because you are the one doing all the organising. People will be happy to follow your lead and the lunar high offers you great power over life generally. Make the most of it and go for something you have wanted to do for a long time.

5 WEDNESDAY ☿ *Moon Age Day 28* *Moon Sign Scorpio*

Your personality dominates the scene today and you may be inclined to push your ideas forward, even when it is quite obvious that some people do not agree with you. If things begin to go wrong at any stage the last thing you should do is to panic. Simply regroup and start again, slowly and steadily.

6 THURSDAY ☿ *Moon Age Day 29* *Moon Sign Scorpio*

The quickened pace of life keeps you on your toes and you begin to enjoy diverse interests to a greater extent. You won't simply be looking in one direction for the answers you need but in many. People generally should seem to be quite helpful and your increased ability to co-operate is part of the reason they are so approachable.

7 FRIDAY *Moon Age Day 0* *Moon Sign Sagittarius*

This is a time to be sorting out basic issues ahead of the Christmas period and for deciding what your plans are going to be. Try not to overcrowd your schedule or else instead of benefiting from the upcoming holiday period you risk ending up fatigued. Jettison a few redundant ideas and try to move forward in your thinking.

8 SATURDAY *Moon Age Day 1* *Moon Sign Sagittarius*

Your independent mental approach and the way you solve problems makes you popular to have around and is the reason why so many people are likely to be turning to you for advice throughout most of today and in the near future. Part of the reason is that you are thinking on your feet and you ooze confidence.

9 SUNDAY *Moon Age Day 2* *Moon Sign Capricorn*

Whilst you might consider that your tendency to speak out and to tell the truth is a positive thing, it is likely that others will not. There are times when a little sugar on the pill is to be recommended and you won't get far today if those closest to you see your attitude as being somewhat brutal. Tact is important so don't forget to use it.

10 MONDAY *Moon Age Day 3   Moon Sign Capricorn*

It is likely that you will be very communicative today and that you will be on the ball when it comes to making little changes at work that can make all the difference in the long-term. Not everyone will be on your side, either professionally or socially but when the chips are down there are many you can rely on.

11 TUESDAY *Moon Age Day 4   Moon Sign Aquarius*

You have so many ideas at the moment it is going to be difficult to get the majority of them off the ground before Christmas period. Certain issues will have to be kept on hold until next year and although this can be frustrating on one level, on another it makes you more excited about the potential for the future.

12 WEDNESDAY *Moon Age Day 5   Moon Sign Aquarius*

There seems to be a great deal of ego and assertiveness around at the moment and at least some of it is coming from your direction. You could be looking towards a period of very hard work and it won't help if you cause problems with the people who can best help you. A little humility now goes a long way.

13 THURSDAY *Moon Age Day 6   Moon Sign Aquarius*

With present trends around you might have to be slightly more frugal than you had been expecting. Perhaps you haven't got everything you need for Christmas yet, whilst at the same time money is short. With a little careful planning you can do what is necessary in terms of gifts whilst spending little and also having fun.

14 FRIDAY *Moon Age Day 7   Moon Sign Pisces*

You crave physical comforts now and will be enlisting the support of loved ones in order to make sure this is possible. Luxury appeals to you, and you won't want to be putting yourself out any more than is strictly necessary. Because you are so loveable it is likely that you receive all the attention you desire.

15 SATURDAY
Moon Age Day 8   Moon Sign Pisces

You are very generous at the moment and that's a good thing, not least of all because you get back much more than you give in one way or another. This would be a good time to enter competitions and to test your skill against others. Social trends are particularly interesting and remain so for some time.

16 SUNDAY
Moon Age Day 9   Moon Sign Pisces

With the accent now firmly on enjoyable communication, you are really looking forward to what Christmas has to offer. For many of you the festive season starts right now and you will be getting into the right frame of mind. Keep an eye on a family member who might have been out of sorts recently.

17 MONDAY
Moon Age Day 10   Moon Sign Aries

You seem to have lots of ideas at your disposal. Even if eight out of ten of them are not workable, that still leaves two that are worth pursuing. With only a few days left until Christmas actually starts, your mind tends to travel back to previous times. There may be a few lessons to be learned from the past.

18 TUESDAY
Moon Age Day 11   Moon Sign Aries

A friendly word in the right ear might make it easy for you to settle a personal issue that has been on your mind. At the same time you can be of significant assistance to colleagues, friends and even your partner. Scorpio is presently at its most co-operative, which enhances your natural popularity.

19 WEDNESDAY
Moon Age Day 12   Moon Sign Taurus

Look out for a little tension that is brought about by the arrival of the lunar low. Such is the speed of your life at the moment that you may almost fail to notice the restrictions that the Moon in Taurus is going to place upon you, though by tomorrow you may be more inclined to feel the brakes being applied.

20 THURSDAY   *Moon Age Day 13   Moon Sign Taurus*

Your fortunes are likely to be in the doldrums but it is unlikely that any major problem is going to emerge. On the contrary you remain generally resilient, even if you have to undertake the same job more than once. Keep your money in your purse or wallet for today and try not to spend more than you have to until a little later.

21 FRIDAY   *Moon Age Day 14   Moon Sign Gemini*

This will most likely be a fairly uneventful and easy-going sort of day and leaves you with plenty of time to lay down those last-minute plans for all that lies ahead of you in the next week or two. Don't allow anyone to push you into any sort of scheme that you don't approve of or about which you have suspicions.

22 SATURDAY   *Moon Age Day 15   Moon Sign Gemini*

Family gatherings ought to be of real interest now and you will be doing more than most to make these possible. Even if you do not come from a very close family background you are likely to feel more attached than usual. A sense of place and belonging is extremely important to you at present.

23 SUNDAY   *Moon Age Day 16   Moon Sign Cancer*

This is a good time during which to try your hand at money making and innovative enterprises. Help with these is certain if you ask around and people generally seem to want to assist you today. There is a quieter side to your nature that shows later but in the main you are happy to be in the social mainstream.

24 MONDAY   *Moon Age Day 17   Moon Sign Cancer*

The arrival of Christmas Eve may bring you much closer to something you have wanted for ages. This should also be a good day for expressing your emotions and for getting onside with your partner. New personalities are likely to enter your life under the social influences of today and you could even make a new friend for life.

25 TUESDAY   *Moon Age Day 18   Moon Sign Leo*

If Christmas Day fails to bring you your heart's desire it won't be far away. There are a multitude of good planetary aspects surrounding you at the present time and these should conspire to offer you a good time. You need to be in the company of people you love in order to make the most of what is on offer.

26 WEDNESDAY   *Moon Age Day 19   Moon Sign Leo*

Change and diversity is important for Boxing Day and although you may have stuck around the homestead yesterday you are far less likely to do so today. Your powers of persuasion are at a peak so if there is someone you now want to influence, you could hardly pick a better time than this to turn on the charm and to convince them.

27 THURSDAY   *Moon Age Day 20   Moon Sign Virgo*

You may now get an opportunity to improve your mind in some way, as well as to learn that you are smarter than you might have thought. You love to pit your wits against those of interesting people, whilst at the same time showing the distinctly competitive edge to your Scorpio nature.

28 FRIDAY   *Moon Age Day 21   Moon Sign Virgo*

As the holidays progress, look out for a few limitations today as far as your own mind is concerned because you seem to be entering a short phase of relative uncertainty. Gains come today as a result of the generosity of those around you, particularly that of family members.

29 SATURDAY   *Moon Age Day 22   Moon Sign Libra*

Daily life might be subject to sudden changes and that could mean having to think on your feet a good deal today. Although you will be comfortable at home, it's possible you will be taking some time out to visit relatives and the change of scenery could work to your advantage.

30 SUNDAY   *Moon Age Day 23   Moon Sign Libra*

This is a great time for communicating well with others. Few people will be at work at the moment but those who are can forge a special bond with colleagues. Ignore the winter weather because it's clear that you need some fresh air in your lungs. Those of you who are away for Christmas probably benefit the most.

31 MONDAY   *Moon Age Day 24   Moon Sign Libra*

There is no doubt that you are on great form today. You could gain new insight into a subject that is currently uppermost in your mind. Not everyone seems to be on the same wavelength as you but by the end of the day you have plenty of energy and can really enjoy what New Year gatherings have to offer.

30 SUNDAY

31 MONDAY

RISING SIGNS FOR SCORPIO

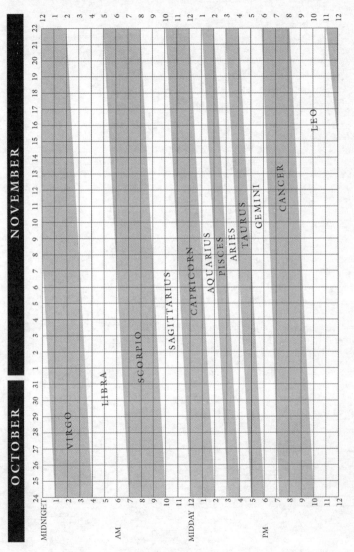

157